Profane culture

Profane culture

Paul E. Willis

Routledge & Kegan Paul
London, Henley and Boston

First published in 1978
by Routledge & Kegan Paul Ltd
39 Store Street,
London WC1E 7DD,
Broadway House,
Newtown Road,
Henley-on-Thames,
Oxon RG9 1EN and
9 Park Street,
Boston, Mass. 02108, USA
Photoset in 11 on 12 Garamond
by Kelly and Wright, Bradford-on-Avon, Wiltshire
and printed in Great Britain by
Lowe & Brydone Ltd

ISBN 0 7100 8789 6

to Joe and Les

Contents

Preface

This book is based on work for my PhD thesis awarded in December 1972. Some of the theoretical strands of that thesis have been taken up by myself and others elsewhere.[1] I have not attempted to recover that development in this text. Instead I have presented as clearly and simply as possible only those basic ideas which are vital for the appreciation of the cultures I describe.

The specific academic discipline from which the book arises is that of Cultural Studies. With all the usual disclaimers thanks to Richard Hoggart and especially to Stuart Hall. They may not agree with, and are certainly not reponsible for, but encouraged me to produce, what follows. Thanks also to others who have read and commented upon drafts of the book: John Clarke, Tony Jefferson, Stuart Laing, Roger Crimshaw, Richard Dyer, Jonathan Benthall, Geoffrey Haydon, Andrew Tolson, Pam Taylor, Terry Dunham, Jeff Nuttall and Dorothy Hobson. Thanks also to those who typed up endless manuscripts and transcriptions: Freda Tooth, Joan Palmer, Pat Berry, Zana Hoskin, Janet Pigott and Wendy Rigg.

Although all those quoted or reported in this book gave full consent to the research, and understood that publication might be forthcoming, all clubs, places, pubs and names of individuals have been changed. My greatest thanks to them.

. . . music alone awakens in man the sense of music. . . . The forming of the five senses is a labour of the entire history of the world down to the present.

Karl Marx, 1844
(*Economic and Philosophic Manuscripts*)

1 Introduction:
Profanity and creativity

The sheer surprise of a living culture is a slap to reverie. Real, bustling, startling cultures move. They exist. They are something in the world. They suddenly leave behind – empty, exposed, ugly – *ideas* of poverty, deprivation, existence and culture. Real events can save us much philosophy.

This book presents two important cultures generated during the 1960s and still widely influential today – the motor-bike boys, sometimes known as rockers, and the hippies, sometimes known as heads or freaks. The form of the book is of two ethnographic accounts of the inner meanings, style and movement of these cultures, but the essential theme of the book is that oppressed, subordinate or minority groups can have a hand in the construction of their own vibrant cultures and are not merely dupes: the fall guys in a social system stacked overwhelmingly against them and dominated by capitalist media and commercial provision. Not only this, but their *profane* creativity shows us the only route for radical *cultural* change. In particular they mark out the aridity of abstract or purely theoretical solutions. It is only real people at work on real objects in an uncertain world who actually produce new movements in style, consciousness and feeling – new arts in life.

 The oppression of working-class youth, the alienation of middle-class youth, can be analysed. The social sciences show the oppression and share the alienation. They outline 'the problem'. They say something must give, something must happen. But it is only in the factories, on the streets, in the bars, in the dance halls, in the tower flats, in the two-up-and-two-downs that contradictions and problems are *lived through* to particular outcomes. It is in these places where direct experience, ways of living, creative acts and penetrations –

1

cultures – redefine problems, break the stasis of meaning, and reset the possibilities somewhat for all of us. And this material[1] experience has not had the benefit of prior validation, of collective discussion, of the security of the common line. It is embedded in the real engagement of experience with the world: in the *dialectic* of cultural life. This is not to say that living cultures do not 'know' the nature of the conditions which produced them. They 'know' them, however, not in words, but in their structures, form and style. They 'know' them as the unsaid precondition for certain kinds of behaviour, as the only possible if silent context which make particular repertoires of action and interest mean anything at all. Not only this, but they 'know' what surrounds them sufficiently to seize and creatively exploit aspects of it to express their own zest and identity – so partially changing their conditions of existence. This is, precisely the *dialectic* of cultural life.

The social sciences could never produce a bedizened, solid motor-bike, an embroidered sheepskin coat, an outrageous rock 'n' roll record. Yet these things speak most profoundly to an age,[2] as vulgar theories damage it. They are the astonishing products of one real outcome when many were contesting, when there were a thousand possibilities. They show us the real movement of experience in the concrete world. Life is the laboratory. Life is the thing. Ethnography is not simply description, it's about capturing that.

Culture, then, is not simply about a relationship with what is called 'art', or with 'the best which has been thought and said', or with the restricted or the refined. I see cultural experience essentially as shared material experience. It does not proceed either from individual variation and proclivity, or from the specifications downwards of a gigantic social order. It comes from direct involvement with the everyday world. It is in relation to the commonplace, to trivia and the slow accumulation of concrete lessons that individuals *in groups*, come to recognize their subjectivity. The determinations of the wider social system are borne in upon the social individual in a thousand different and variable ways. Tastes, feelings, likes and dislikes are developed in minute articulation with the concrete world.

The essential and primitive distinction I wish to make is not an idealist one between 'art' and 'non-art', but between two types of human involvement with this world: between a random or arbitrary relationship, and a reciprocal, or, as I have called it, *dialectical* relationship. All material experience is a complex combination of both, but we need to separate them in thought in order to take a grip on what is distinctive in new cultural forms.

Random relationships, though a 'fact of nature' and necessary for survival perhaps, are not only unintended from the point of view of the group experiencing them, but do not express anything of particular internal importance or relevance. There is no creative articulation of meaning through a *responsive* field of external items. Commodity production continuously expands the field of items for such relationships. It provides toothpaste, spanners, cans of beans, roads, tower blocks and all the glitter of the new consciousness/cultural industry.

In the long term such random relations act to condition subjectivity in a way which is beyond the control of the individual or group. This is one of the profoundest meanings of domination. The deadliest domination comes through the domination of trivia. This book, however, considers this level in another light. It examines how people – uncertainly, through unforeseen consequence and often without consciousness or purpose – take at least a hand in their own day-to-day making. We will look at two minority and excluded cultures whose forms look random and arbitrary from the outside and incapable of expressing any significant internal cultural meanings, to judge how far their central relationships are actually reciprocal, expressive and developmental. These cultures are important and full of lessons for us because the things of the world which surround them, and through which they are developed and expressed, are without conventional 'cultural' or 'artistic' significance. These cultures work through profane materials: simple functional commodities, drugs, chemicals and cultural commodities exploitatively produced by the new 'consciousness industry'. And yet from the rubbish available within a preconstituted market these groups do generate viable cultures, and through their work on received

3

commodities and categories, actually formulate a living, lived out and concretized critique of the society which produces these distorted, insulting, often meaningless things. After the main ethnographic accounts, further chapters explore the particular relationship of both cultures to their most important constitutive material items: the motor-bike and rock 'n' roll for the motor-bike boys, drugs and progressive music for the hippies.

The essence of the cultural relationship I explore in these chapters is that certain items in the cultural field of a social group come to closely parallel its structure of feeling and characteristic concerns.[3] Having posited itself, shown its existence, manifested an identity in concrete worldly items, the social group has a degree of conscious and unconscious security. It does not have the same struggle with the void of possibilities its culture and identity might have been. And with this stored and coded image safely locked up within cultural items the social group can then, in a reverse dialectical moment, learn from and be influenced by its own cultural field and develop its feelings, attitudes and taste in relation to perhaps a widening circle of art forms, cultural items and objects – in particular directions first instituted by itself and its own needs. Thus internally modified, the social group can then further choose new objects, select or change the originals, so as to reset the struture and form of its cultural field – and so institute a further confirming circuit of the *dialectic*. It is in this process of mutual adaption and selection that particular cultural items come at all to resemble the structure and form of the social group, so to speak, in the first place.

This is not necessarily to place consciousness and human will at the centre of the stage, or to imply that specific cultural forms or activities are the result of the conscious purpose of particular social groups.[4] The form of exchange between the social group and its cultural field might be at many levels. Some may be conscious, others unconscious, many unintended and finally surprising to the participants. Not only the materials, but the course and development of a culture may be unspecified, not prefigured in any rule book and finally profane. Furthermore those things which are reflected and expressed in the cultural field relate to the position of the social group in the social

4

structure. They may be unpleasant or specifically repressed from the consciousness of the group. Cultural expressions are even likely to be displaced, distorted or condensed reflections of barely understood, or 'misunderstood', knots of feeling, contradiction and frustration – as well as forms of action on these things. It is this degree of specificity which means we can learn from them. We learn from the culture, not from its explicit consciousness.

It is clear from this view of culture that the dominant class in society has certain profound advantages. It has the greatest access to 'culture' and the greatest agency with which to change and modify items in its cultural field. Its members have greater time and money to develop their sensibilities, and they control the basic institutions which maintain the society, and the position of their class within it, as well as the daily context of their detailed lives. All this is to be recognized, but if they are mainly the beneficiaries of capitalism, they are also partly its victims. The dominant class is most victim to the illusions and false promises of its own ideology. What looks like the last gift of privilege – cultural attainment and a living sensual involvement with the world – turns out to be its opposite: stultification, reification and pretence. The conflation of art and culture with social élitism and exclusion[5] leads to conformist hesitancy and the minimum strategy of knowing the accepted wisdom. Despite their objective privilege and their power in material production of all kinds, the dominant class is least suited to see and explore the unexpected, the double edge, the revolutionary in what it produces.

It is the worst productions out of the dead hand of the market which surround oppressed and minority groups: what capitalism has rejected, thrown aside, thoughtlessly produced or carelessly sustained to keep the cynical commercial penny turning. But because they are surrounded by plastic ersatz and the detritus of the bourgeoisie, there is for all that a more desperate need not to be duped, but to find meaning and potential within what they find[6] – they have nothing else. And in certain respects their eyes are clearer. For all the shit, there is a freedom in the market, on the streets, in the pubs and in the dance halls. And what is provided cynically for the profit of others and not for the benefit of the individual at least avoids certain kinds of moral over-rides. There is no restrictive embrace implicit in the social conventions of valuing something not for itself, but for the exclusion it brings. Though the whole commodity form provides powerful implications for the ,,manner of its consumption, it by no means enforces them. ¡Commodities can be taken out of context, claimed in a particular way, developed and repossessed to express something deeply and thereby to change somewhat the very feelings which are their product.[7] And all this can happen under the very nose of the dominant class – and with their products.

We might even say that the characteristic of a certain kind of creative cultural development is the exploitation of qualities, capacities and potentials in those profane things which the dominant society has thrown aside, produced 'as business', or left undeveloped for cultural meaning. Despite their appalling and deprived location and despite the huge advantages of the dominant class, it is sometimes the dispossessed who are best placed to exploit the revolutionary double edge of unexplored things around us. It is the acid of profane cultures which eats away the bourgeois scales from the commonplace.

This is a grand claim. In fact the years since the high points of the 1960s cultural upheaval make indulgence and romanticism less a danger. Despite their achievements, and the potentials they indicate, the hippy and bike cultures introduced no lasting change. Perhaps what we should learn is at a level of theory and example: ways of thinking through cultural change for the next time. It is much clearer now that both cultures reproduced – even creatively – the weaknesses, brutality and limitations of their own structural locations and parent class cultures. There can no longer be any false elision between their creative achievements in a particular determinate context and larger programmes for change or even challenge to society. Not only this, but the very fullness and boldness of their cultural commitment and working through of problems and perspectives at the level of life-style engendered its own massive and tragic failure: an inability to break from cultural forms into any kind of political activity or power struggle to change or challenge the main institutions of society, patterns, of work, vested interests or the most basic organization of the social classes. The cultures did not secure the conditions for their own continuance or the modification of those brutalizing and repressive determinations which made them, in the first place, what they were; struggling as the weaker partner. These basic limitations are more obvious now, and bring out in the cultures, increasingly an air of tragedy and fatalism evident in certain central dynamics down to the disorganization and suffering of particular individuals.

Still these cultures teach us that revolutionary cultural change will only come from reinterpretations, reformations of consciousness, and fermentation from below around the most trivial, everyday and commonplace items. Such change cannot be simply provided from above, or from ideas. It is not a matter of reorganizing the same pieces. It is not just a question of the big armies. It concerns thinking and feeling and how things are seen: new eyes on old objects. Big change is no change unless it changes the small: our commonsense beings, commonplace habits, and accepted use of everyday objects. Cultural change must have the profanity of daring the world – not its ideas. We must listen to the streets before we listen at the towers.

The hippies and bikeboys were in the struggles of the 1960s. They were not bystanders. They produced something. We can look at it and learn from it.

The two cultures presented in this book are quite different. Their choice was not, however, random. They share many things.

They were both minority cultures and existed in material conditions which would be described conventionally as deprived. Of course this was, to some extent, voluntary in the case of the hippies. They were modern apostates. They turned their backs on the supposed material and cultural advantages of a middle-class life-style. The motor-bike boys were, on the other hand, the uncalled. They had no choice about their socio-economic circumstances.

They also both existed in a crucially modern world. This is a world which is post Elvis Presley, and post the controversy about the 'generation gap'. Both groups are deeply involved in the appreciation of forms of pop music, and understand something of the wider symbolic articulations of the pop world. In their different ways, the cultures represent, in fact, twin high peaks in the short history of pop music. The motor-bike boys liked early rock 'n' roll of the 1950s – the generally accredited golden age of pop: the hippies were involved in the post-Beatles high point of 'progressive' music.

Though the actual form of their preferred music is very different, both cultures arise in the post-McLuhan world of telecommunications. Music was relayed and enjoyed only because of the advances in telecommunications and electronics. The characteristic form of appreciation is of music which is recorded and depends on the precise configuration of voice and backing. The ascendancy of pop music marked the decline of sheet music as the main distributed form of popular music. Sheet music could be played in very different ways by different groups at different times. The essence of music, the common denominator between groups, was the notation on the sheet. In the age of pop music, the only text is the actual record. This makes the precise style and intonation of the singer very important, so that the same song by a different singer is a completely different artefact. This ability of telecommunications to displace the formal written mode allows a real immediacy between singer and audience even though vastly separated socially and geographically. It opens up all kinds of possibilities for a new idiom shared simultaneously across disparate communities. In their different ways both cultures benefited from this.

The main difference between the cultures is, of course, in their locating parent cultures. The motor-bike boys were broadly from the working class, and the hippies broadly from the middle class. They are similar, however, in representing for us the most durable, extreme, creative variants of these class cultures within the youth-cultural mode. The motor-bike boys were exploring and extending versions of 'rough' working-class themes. The hippies were exploring and broadening a middle-class tradition of the bohemian intelligentsia – especially as drawn into the lumpen or déclassé urban milieu. It is possible to suggest that all other distinctive life-styles lie somewhere between these two in terms of their class-cultural nature and location. They can, to some extent, be thought out in terms of these extremes.

Part one

He used to have a rocket, you know, this mate of mine. You know, and I felt sick when I heard he'd died, 'cause we'd had some good times, you know, and I felt sick. I had a dream about it, you know. In heaven St Peter is there, and there's a dirty great big open road . . . there's nothing coming this way, you know, just that way, and you're going really fast, you know, like a figment of your imagination, you know, ordinarily it would have blown you off, you're going so fast, it's such a fast bike. . . . no cars, no motor-scooters, nothing like that, just motor-bikes and every now and again there's a café, about every fifteen miles or so . . . and the coffee's free, and the music's playing . . . rock music, it'd be rock 'n' roll, all those Bill Haley, Little Richard, you know. All the ones I like, all the ones I've got and I still like, they'd all be on, in every café I go to, you know . . . and there's all blonde virgins waiting for you, and all the coffee's free, and the music's playing, and there's just one dirty great big highway all to yourself, and St Peter gives you a bike to ride and try . . . so it must be great up there, honest. . . . Just go in the café, quick coffee and 'wham', on to the big highway again, no bends, nothing coming the other way . . . after all this I think I'm going to die tonight when I get on the bike.

Joe, 1969

2 The motor-bike boys

1 The approach

I made contact with a motor-bike club in a large English city in 1969, and continued field work and interviews there over a period of nine months. The club is now closed and the members disbanded. During the period of 'the research' the club was very successful, and always full, and had an official membership in the hundreds. The boys were in the typical style of the motor-bike boy, or 'rocker', or 'greaser'.[1] Studded leather jackets and greasy denim jeans were the norm. Large motor-cycle boots or large marching boots were worn on the feet. Hair was normally long and greasy, swept back with a small quiff at the front. The leather jackets were frequently adorned with badges and mottoes.

Though this group and style was clearly marked out during the 1960s by their opposition – accomplished partly through the media[2] – to the 'mods', the culture still exists today. The style represents one basic form of working-class culture as it is lived by the young, and contains – often in highly explicit forms – central continuing working-class themes and values.

I spent a few evenings simply 'hanging around' the club and taking in its general atmosphere. Contacts could be made with members through the full-time official. One of these contacts, Mick, a long-standing member and one-time secretary to the club, was sympathetic and introduced me to his particular group of friends. These friends, ranging in age from late teens to middle 20s, were not involved in the formal structure of the club, and strongly resisted its latent functions of social control, although they had attended regularly over a number of years.

11

Over the next few weeks, I developed a kind of relationship with this group and finally suggested that they might like to listen to records, and discuss their reactions and whatever else interested them on tape. They agreed – and certainly out of no obligation or coercion. It was frequently impossible to get them all together at one time, and I often spent the evening just drifting around the club chatting here and there or generally observing things. It should be remembered that my study was of the larger social and cultural whole and not of a specific group or of specific individuals except in so far as they embodied central meanings and values. I was not perturbed by this randomness of contact. *General* exposure to the culture was of the utmost importance.

A typical evening for the motor-bike boys would consist of permutations of the same activities: a coffee in the coffee bar, a drink and a game of darts in the local pub, a game of table-tennis or pin-ball in the coffee bar, general horseplay around the premises, chatting in groups around the club. The social situation was very fluid and Mick's group would not remain a coherent whole, but split up and mixed generally about the club. The composition of the group with which I taped discussions also changed over time and varied in number. It centrally included Mick (a foundry worker), Joe (a scaffolder), Fred (a scaffolder), Tim (a milkman), Percy (a student), Roger (unemployed) and Sue (unemployed, girlfriend of Joe). Percy and Roger were not part of Mick's group of friends, but joined our discussions on a few occasions, and were always around the club and well known to all its members.

Sometimes it was possible, usually in the pub at about the middle of the evening, to suggest to whomever was around from 'the group' and sometimes others that we should go to one of the committee rooms for half an hour to play and discuss particular records. I would play a number of records both of my own and of their choice, and ask them their opinions. These sessions were relatively unstructured and the discussions frequently 'took off' in unpredictable directions without any prompting from me.

Although by no means fully accepted I think I was a guy who was known to be 'ok', if a little grey and detached. A lot of the time I was simply unnoticed. That my interest in their culture was general and based also on their music, rather than on them directly, helped to minimize distrust or awkwardness.

The following account is based on general observation, conversations with individuals and groups, participation around the club, often with the group described above, and tape-recorded sessions.

2 Security of identity

The world of the motor-bike boys was above all else concrete and unequivocal. They perceived it without ontological insecurity, without existential angst. Words like that did not exist. There was no space for them. Values, attitudes and feelings were so deeply entrenched as to form part of an obvious commonsense reality. There was no abstract dimension to the world, no guilty reading, no burdened 'I' – just a straightforward physicality and confidence in things. The touchstones of this world were manliness, toughness and directness of interpersonal contact.

Frankness and directness characterized all of their social interaction. Formal structures or considerations of politeness did not distort normal ongoing life. Form and style were located in concrete and lived situations, not in books on etiquette. Status in any kind of outside hierarchical structure was ignored so far as their relations with each other were concerned. They lived in the unreified world of the present and its immediate relations.

An element of the informality and directness of the world in which they lived was the widespread use of nicknames. These nicknames were partly given by the group and partly adopted by the individual. Once the nicknames were coined they were used universally, and it was difficult to find out what real names were.

Self-reliance and identity

The motor-bike boys relied directly on the strength and control of their own agency. This was shown by their attitude towards drugs. They were hated not revered. They were not seen (as was the motor-bike, for instance) as the unformed material of excitement, glamour or new experience. They were seen as a threat to the integrity of individual agency, as a threat to the ability to act and make decisions autonomously. The drug-pusher's needle of uncertainty picks loose the main thread of the motor-bike boy's life: self-reliance:

PW:	Drugs?
Fred:	Oh, fucking drugs, that's stupid. . . .
Several voices:	Yeah, it's stupid . . . yeah.
Fred:	I've never taken a drug in my fucking life, I'd punch the fuck out of the kid who offered me one.
PW:	Would you?
Fred:	Yeah, I would.
Mick:	And I would.
Tim:	They can't be men if they take drugs . . . there must be something wrong with them.
Sue:	Stupid, ain't it?
Fred:	If I knew anyone that took them, I'd fucking do 'em.
Mick:	If I couldn't do anything without a drug in me, I wouldn't want to do it at all.
Fred:	If I took something to make me fucking do it, I wouldn't want to know.
Mick:	It's the same as beer, isn't it. I mean you get a lot of people, they've got to have a drink before they'll bleeding hit anybody. If I couldn't hit anybody without any beer or drugs . . . I wouldn't be much.
Fred:	I know a lot of kids, they go and have a lot of booze, before they go and have a tattoo or something, they're scared of having it, I mean without beer, it's a drug that is, isn't it.
Sue:	It's ridiculous, it's Dutch courage.

It is interesting that alcohol is immediately classed with 'drugs', although it has a very different social characterization. The point is this: they are not concerned with fine gradations between different drugs. They understand 'drugs' in a global fashion.

They are seen as loosening up the strict relationship between consciousness and reality, between decision and action in the world, between thought and concrete expression. They have never tried 'drugs' apart from alcohol and did not know the grammar of depressant, stimulant, hallucinogen. They had no experiential or analytic basis for their views. Rather the basis of their feeling was a deep-rooted fear. The commonsense and obvious nature of the physical and social world was at once the basis of their reality and the source of their identity. It was the here and now within which their meanings were worked, which expressed *them*. Dissociation not only questioned reality, it questioned their identity. Extinction, or dissolution of the concrete world, was not a matter of philosophic or abstract interest as it was in the drug experience: it was the dissolution of personality. The boys did not want their consciousness surreptitiously set free from apparent substantiality to slip behind, and question, their reality and ultimately their identity.

Death and identity

The motor-bike was the crucial symbolic piece of the bike culture.[3] Death on the motor-bike was very common.[4] Their fascination with such a death was frequently expressed:

Fred:	Racing coppers.
Joe:	Hoorah!
Fred:	Get two of them behind, all fucking day. Thunderbolts, you know, the coppers' thunderbolts, and you're fucking pissing away on an export bonnie or sommat, give it almighty stick, you know, and you kick a couple of coppers, so fast, smoking, your tyres are set alight you know, and a fucking great big twenty-ton lorry comes across, an artic, and you go up the back.
Joe:	Like up the Junction?
Fred:	No, like Johnny Gibson, oh he did fucking hell, he did, blood poured from everywhere, cracked his fucking skull wide open.

The motor-bike boys

The interest in the motor-bike could be taken to signify a morbid fascination with death, paralleling, in a sense, the search for excitement and new experience through drugs. This would be to misunderstand the relationship of the bike boys to the motor-bike. The skills of handling a motor-bike were widely valued, and were precisely about *avoiding* unnecessary accident. To have died through obvious incompetence, would not have been meaningful. Their attitude was not one of submission to the motor-bike, but one of assertion which stressed the importance of *control*. If the machine would not be subjugated by their will, then it was to be distrusted, not valued:

Fred: No . . . the motor-bike don't frighten you.
Joe: If the bike handles well, the bike will never
               beat you; if it handles bad, it frightens you,
               that's all.
PW: Frightens – what does 'frightens' mean?
Joe: No, scared, I mean. Like if I've got a bike,
               and it don't handle well, I won't go fast on
               it; but if it'll do everything you want it to,
               well that's it you know.

It is precisely, therefore, confidence in the controllability, the unequivocality, of the physical world which expands to envelop and control the ferocity of the motor-bike – not vice versa.

Not only is the ontological security of the motor-bike boys demonstrated in their mastery of the motor-bike, but the qualities and function of the machine itself express their sense of concrete identity within an unarguable reality. The motor-bike responds inevitably and concretely to the subjective will, it accelerates to the point of blowing the rider off at the twist of a wrist. Control decisions are met immediately by the physical consequences of rushing air. The sheer mechanical functioning of the motor-bike – the engineered hardness of metal against metal, the minutely controlled explosion of gases, the predictable power from the swing of machined components – underwrites a positive and durable view of the physical world. Abstraction shrinks in the mouth of technology.

Even danger on the bike was accepted matter-of-factly in the scope of a fully connected consciousness. Nor was death regarded in a loose romantic or adventurist fashion. The

16

motor-bike death was a highly specific affirmation of important *lived* values. Those values concerned not transcendentalism, but precisely the capable handling of a bike: the mastery of a powerful alien technology. Death through stupidity held no value. The significant death came only after physical limits had been pushed to the full, after the body had made massive attempts to control, after the boundaries of skill had been passed, when the rider could do nothing more to save himself. That was 'the way to go': at the point of maximum exertion and skill. It summed up, glorified and held eternally for a second all the aspects of riding a fast bike well – those qualities which in fact, paradoxically, make death less likely in the normal course.

The significance of death for the motor-bike boys is, therefore, very much in *this* world, and not in any mystical 'other' world. At no point is consciousness, or the incontrovertibility of material things, challenged: even in the prospect of death, the risk is met in the confidence and expectation of full consciousness. Death is not an anodyne, but paradoxically, the quintessential recognition of awareness and personality.

What is often regarded as a fatalism or a knowing wager with death is, for the motor-bike boys, in fact the specific evocation of the *unexpected, uncontrollable* and *unlooked* for event, which comes at the moment of *greatest* skill. No fore-knowledge, no after-knowledge, is to be allowed into their freezing of a moment: a moment of control central to their *living* culture:

Fred: As I say, if I knew I was going to die, you know going down the road on a bike, I wouldn't go down the fucking road on the bike, that's it, I wouldn't purposely go out and get killed as I say.

Fred: Just blast down the road giving it almighty stick, and fucking that's it. I don't want to know I was going to die, you know what I mean, but if I was going to die, I wouldn't mind going on a bike – fucking great.

Joe: It's the way you do it, that's all.

Fred: I'd like to die racing down the road, down

17

the bastard, give it almighty stick, give a jag
a go, and then, you know, a fucking big
lorry comes out, crunch, that's the end of
you . . . nice, eh?

3 The style of identity

This absolute security of identity was characteristically expressed
in a distinctive style. There was a rumbustious extroversion, a
rough bonhomie, sometimes a bravado, that shot through their
social relations. Their sense of security was enacted through an
essentially masculine style.

Physicality of interaction

At a simple physical level and certainly by conventional
standards, the motor-bike boys were rough and tough. Many
social exchanges were conducted in the form of mock fights,
with pushing, mock punches, sharp karate-type blows to the
back of the neck. They were also rough with inanimate objects.
There were pin-tables in the coffee bars. If one of the tables
were broken and not working, a crowd of boys would start to
take it to pieces to try and repair it. They would get so far and
then start thumping and banging it, lifting it bodily from the
floor and dropping it. This did not usually produce results, and
after giving it a good 'cussing out', and a few good kicks, they
would forget about it. A small example, but it does
demonstrate their tough and immediate approach to problems.
Science and careful analysis might be tried for a while but unless
this produced results quickly, it was discarded for rough direct
measures: the attempt literally to kick things into shape with
the confidence of a crude masculine strength. When this too
failed, the whole project was dismissed, not in the way of
failure, but in the way of masculine disdain – 'fuck it'.
Masculinity, from confidence in raw strength, to aggressive
disdain, provided a continuity, and a mode of confronting
complex reality which allowed for a dignified and unruffled
passage through potentially awkward situations: a passage from
outright confrontation to lordly disdain.

18

I did not see this rough style develop into actual violence. The boys had, however, been in several fights and spoke of the occasions with some enjoyment. Mick had been a Teddy boy in his earlier years and had been involved in several fights during that period. He could never understand why so many people seemed to 'take objection' to him, and why he was so often 'forced' into fighting. It was true of them all that they came to the club because other clubs, and often public cafés, would not have them. Quite apart from personal violence there was, of course, as we have seen, the danger to equipment. The stories of previous violence were often taken as material for a boisterous humour:

PW:	There are plenty of other clubs around, why this one?
Mick:	Well, we used to box for him, you know, and we were practising one night . . . one night, and we just got into trouble and got kicked out.
PW:	You mean you hit someone?
Fred:	Fucking John jumped out of the ring with his gloves on, and started to fight everyone. (Laughter.)

Dislike of others was immediately interpreted in terms of violence to those disliked. 'Mods', or what they understood to be mods, were a group that attracted particularly violent responses. Several of them said that they had attempted to ride scooters (the 'mod' form of transport) off the road, or cause them to take evasive action designed to cause an accident. A clear territorial sense about their club was backed up with the threat of violence:

Fred:	If you allowed the scooters to come up here, there wouldn't be much left on them – they'd be smashed up. There wouldn't be much left of them, they wouldn't get out again.
Joe:	If a load of fucking mods came up here, they'd be done.

APPEARANCE

sk8 - street urchin

The masculine style

The motor-bike boys' style was masculine in more developed ways than the simply violent. Their appearance was aggressively masculine. The motor-cycle gear both looked tough, with its leather, studs and denim, and by association with the motor-bike, took over some of the intimidating quality of the machine. Hair was worn long, in a greasy swept-back style, drawing on the connotations of the early Elvis Presley image. The heavy boots were reminiscent of the factory as well as fearsome weapons in a no-holds-barred fight situation. Tattooes on the hands, arms and chest were extremely common; gold rings in pierced ear lobes not uncommon.

It is interesting that the outside group which was hated most, the mods, were despised particularly for their feminine traits, and feminine ways of dressing – implicit contradictions of what was valued by the motor-bike boys in their own culture. In this transcription there is also interesting evidence about how I was seen by the group:

PW:	On the dress, though . . . you wouldn't like it too much if the mods came, would you?
Fred:	No, I'd fucking hate it.
PW:	You thought I was a mod, or somebody thought I was.
Sue:	Yes, we did.
Fred:	You know, there's a mod behind the bar now and I hate the fucking sight of him . . . I hate him . . . he's sly-looking. I don't like them . . . that cunt, fucking Jesus, I hate him. I'd love the cunt to get fucking done.
PW:	Why don't you like the mods?
Fred:	Hmn?
PW:	Why don't you like the mods?
Fred:	A load of cunts, ain't they? Fucking putting their make-up on and all that.
Sue:	Feminine, too feminine.
Fred:	You see them on the bus . . . you only touch them and they fucking fall apart.
Mick:	You know, they think of us as long-haired

> scruffs and . . . they ponce theirselves up a
> bit and they've got short hair and we don't
> care what we wear . . . you see them with
> these trousers with flowers all over them.

Their notion of 'mods' is imprecise. The usual view of the mod gives him shortish, neatly-combed, hair, and neat, well-cut clothes: flowered trousers would have been distinctly *de trop*. Both the 'mod' behind the bar and I were quite different from this. The crucial 'mod' characteristic for them seemed to be what they took as *femininity*. The man behind the bar was in fact more in the fashion of the 'hippy', but the gentleness of this style was taken as femininity, which was identified with the 'mod'.

As for myself, I found in the motor-bike boys' image of me an important insight into the qualities and style of their culture. They saw me as lacking in the ability to initiate action, or to respond in a physical way. Although apparently underpowered, I did have a kind of presence in that I had made contact with the group and kept on coming. Although detached and cool, my interest in their life was taken as a kind of sociability. However, lack of assertiveness, for them, was close to 'cissiness' which was taken as a prime 'mod' characteristic. In the course of my research I met other groups who had quite different, often contradictory, images of me. In a strong and unified culture such as this, impressions are formed about individuals in a way which has more internal than external significance: they speak to the parameters which do the measuring. Some qualities are missed altogether. Other qualities that are in line with esteemed values are picked up very delicately. Essentially, the motor-bike boys were making their reading of others along an exclusively and finely graded masculine/non-masculine scale.

The motor-bike boys' attitude toward Percy[5] was interesting for what it tells us of their masculine style. He was the butt for repeated jokes and innuendoes suggesting his weakness, femininity and even homosexuality. He was repeatedly bullied and accused of imagined misdemeanours. A natural shyness made it difficult for him to handle these situations. His tongue-tied embarrassment was taken as further evidence of his dubious manhood. The following scenario was repeated many times in different forms. One night while some of the boys were collecting in a corner of the church to hear some records, there was from the narrow passageway running up the side of the church a noise of playful shouts and squeals from a group of girls apparently being molested in a rumbustious sort of way. There was laughter from our group and Joe said something such as 'Percy's at it again . . . none of the girls are safe with him around'. All the group laughed and agreed, embellishing the imaginary situation with crude additions of their own. The point of the laughter was, of course, that Percy seemed to them singularly incapable of such a full-blooded male-hunger-type approach. Percy himself joined us in the middle of the situation, and this, to his great perplexity, greatly increased everyone's amusement. They asked him what he'd been doing, and what was the idea of molesting girls in such a way. He denied any part in the event, with great though subdued indignation. The attitude of the group then changed entirely and they accused him of impotency: 'Why, wouldn't you know what to do with them then?' On the one hand he was jokingly accused of a heavy-handed sexual approach, on the other hand he was accused of being incapable precisely of that heavy-handed sexual approach. It was a double bind in which any response from Percy would have met with further derision and rejection. Uncomfortable as it was for Percy, it clearly showed the experimentation with, and mobilization of, group values that were held to be important in the bike culture. In a concentrated way views about the appropriate masculine style had both been aired and substantiated. Rough horseplaying antics, and particularly heavy-handed approaches to women, were approved of, but it was precisely this kind of 'ability' that Percy did not have, and could not have been held to have. Thus the humour at the disjunction between Percy's actual performance, and the imagined scenario of havoc among the women. When it becomes clear that Percy was not involved, and moreover was at pains to dissociate himself (he did not ride with the joke), then he is accused of a failing in masculine feeling. The positive rough encounter with the girls is juxtaposed with the negative of Percy's bloodless, effeminate approach. His failure, and unintended substantiation of the negative stereotype, is twofold. On the one hand it is clear that his reserve makes a rumbustious approach to women impossible, and on the other hand he does not ride with the horseplay of the jokey situation he walks into. It might have been forgivable to have been uninvolved in the playful scuffle in the passage; it was unforgivable not to want to have been. He could have joined in the current of feeling. At least he could have *pretended* to have been there, or showed some enthusiasm for that kind of activity. In his indignant response he doubly strengthened, but in a negative way, the original *point* of the joke. The substance of that joke was about an aggressive masculine style of behaviour.

'Handling yourself'

This style, or ambience, of masculinity is partly caught in the notion of 'handling yourself': of moving quickly and confidently, in a very physical, even intimidating, practical world. Frequently, it was said of a respected figure, 'he can handle himself'. At one level this was the ability or potential ability to 'handle yourself' in a *real* fight situation. At another level, the same physical propensities were symbolically expanded into a rough kind of bonhomie. The bikeboys' interpersonal relationships involved a great deal of physical contact. Movement, and confidence in movement, was the key to their style. I felt an inability to respond fully in such physical relationships. I often felt large and awkward *still* in the midst of action. Conversation was similarly confident and rumbustious – in one way bullying, in another way playful though heavy-handed. Unlike Percy, I could 'ride' such rough good humour as a peripheral member of the group. The elements of spontaneity and unquestioned confidence were, however, missing.

These reactions underline the special kind of tough masculinity, control and confidence through which their secure identity was expressed. It was not easily adopted: it was most basically a cultural expression. That the style and roughness of this 'bonhomie' was a *symbolic* extension of fighting ability, and not a direct extension, is illustrated by the case of the dwarf.

A dwarf used the club regularly. He was much too small to ride a motor-bike and he did not wear motor-bike gear. Clearly he was also much too small to be very effective in a fight situation. However, in a crucial sense he could 'handle himself' and was popular in the club, especially with Mick and Joe. A common form of exchange with the dwarf was the mock fight in which Mick and Joe would go through an elaborate fight routine and suddenly pretend to be overpowered or mortally injured. In this sense their approach to him was similar to their approach to Percy. An amusing situation would be developed by the construction of a scenario which emphasized the gap between real and imagined abilities. The imagined ability was always a culturally-approved-of ability. As well as the mock fights, there were frequent jokes of the sort 'I'll set him on to you' when someone had apparently annoyed one of the motor-bike boys. However, the crucial difference between Percy and the dwarf was that the dwarf went along with these fictions. He would readily stick up his fists, characterize the flashy footwork of a professional boxer, and hit his adversary with what was probably all of his strength. The dramatic downfall of his opponent was greeted with puff-chested pride, strutting, baiting and aggressive shouts worthy of Muhammad Ali. Although the dwarf clearly lacked the physical strength and mastery, he more than made up for this with the symbolic masculinity and rough 'matiness' of his style. Percy, although reasonably well made, and although knowledgeable about motor-bikes, could not deal in this currency, he did not have the same cultural resonance. The baiting of Percy amounted to a kind of cruelty: the jokes about him, although beginning in playfulness, ended with a hardness which was meant, and received, as hurtful. In contrast to this, the jocular treatment of the dwarf was entirely playful, and in the end, protective. The rough masculinity with which the dwarf was treated, was turned, in the end, through an excess of good feeling, into a fatherly protection and support of the dwarf. He was, in a way, the mascot of the motor-bike boys. He could hold and celebrate the values of the motor-bike culture, without the usual accompanying physical threat to usurp the crown. It was this ability to *embody symbolically masculine qualities*, without the *actual* ability to be threatening in the masculine mode, that made him popular and cherished in a way that Percy certainly was not, and even in a way that culturally respected figures such as Joe were not. To have extended this kind of warmth to Joe, may just have resulted in 'having your head punched in' for being too patronizing.

Another example of this kind of rough bonhomie was in the relationship of the motor-bike boys to the publican of 'the local'. A lot of time was spent playing darts in the back-room of this pub. Although, of course, there were clear economic reasons for adapting his behaviour to that of his clientele, this publican was adept at returning the rough kind of bantering humour that the boys dealt in. He was frequently threatened with being 'duffed up'. At some point in the evening, somebody would threaten to 'Climb over the bar and put one on him'. This kind of response was very typically to do with the price of the beer, or some imagined shortcoming in service. However, the threats were only playfully meant, and the publican would return, 'Come on then, climb over and you won't climb back', holding up his fists. A deprecating laugh, or a shared smile, would decisively communicate that the violence was not real, but *part of an accepted mode of interpersonal behaviour*. The bantering, mock fights, threats and pushing were at their most developed at closing time when the publican had the awkward job of closing the back-room with glasses full, and a game of darts in progress. He was always successful in clearing the room, but only with a precise balance of mock bullying, straight appeal, and heavy chauvinist humour such as 'That bird's just gone out, why don't you follow and give her one, eh? – you'd be alright there'. Although the publican was middle-aged and definitely not a motor-bike boy, he had adapted perfectly to at least one dimension of the motor-bike boys' culture.

It should not be taken for granted that this bantering playfulness was completely harmless. It was most harmless when it was returned in like style: when it was clear that the respondent 'knew the game'. When faced with hostility or a serious taking up of apparent challenge, this kind of rough humour could easily develop into a brawl. I never saw such an incident, but the stories from the boys and statements from the club leader and local police supply ample evidence of trouble in pubs and cafés. Many of these places had put a total ban on motor-cycle boys.

This confident masculine style at full stretch amounted to a *bravado*, a larger-than-life playing out of values that constituted a distorted code of honour. For instance, when Joe knew that he was going to jail there was no public feeling of sympathy for him, and he did not seem to expect sympathy. The motor-bike boys had the shadings of a criminal sub-culture: many of them had been in jail at one time or another. Joe had been in jail before. He proudly recounted how it was possible to survive in some comfort. Cigarettes had great importance in jail and were used as a kind of currency. Careful saving, careful dealing and regular supplies from the outside allowed one to become a mini-capitalist through bartering. This gave power, comforts and privileges quite unbelievable to an outsider. This is not to say that Joe was looking forward to jail, but he regarded the prospect with a muscularity and an optimism, at least at the public level, which precluded indulgent feelings of sorrow. It is interesting that Joe came to terms with his future prospects by making at least some aspects of the alienating situation subordinate *to him*. Even though he would be powerless in so many aspects of his life, at least a 'handy' chap like him would operate the cigarette-bartering system to cushion himself against the worst humiliations. This is a transcription from the last discussion including Joe before he went to jail – he was to face the court the following morning. It shows detailed aspects of what I am claiming generally for the culture: bravado in the face of authority; the heavy humour of friends; rough physical interplay, even, or especially, at crucial emotional moments. Here is Joe – incidentally on tape – bidding farewell to his friends for what might be the last time before he goes 'down':

PW:	OK, best of luck tomorrow.
Joe:	See you in six months, tarrah Fred.
Fred:	Oh, my fucking leg, you dirty cunt. [Joe had hit him sharply in the leg while passing on his way to the door.]
Joe:	See you in six months. [Laughter.]
PW:	Can't you beat the charge?
Mick:	Can't you get out for the night?
Joe:	Well, I'll say to the old boy – hey look here, cunt, I want to go down to my club tonight, fucking let me go . . . no I'll say to the

	judge, now listen fucking let me go. . . .
	Come down [to PW] because I might be out
	. . . Monday, I might be out.
PW:	Monday? I hope you are, I really hope you
	are.
All:	Tarrah, cheerio.

Another aspect of their bravado was their frequently stated preference for an early death. The following comments are larger than life, but, bearing in mind the accident record and the real risks taken on the motor-bike, they should not be taken as self-parody or mischievous posing:

Joe:	You'd hate to get old wouldn't you?
Fred:	I'd hate to grow old. I see some old people
	and I think, fuck, if I was like you I'd go
	under the first bus.

Mick:	You wanna go when you're happy, you
	know, walking along on sticks, you need to
	get down the road – you can't call that
	happy.
Fred:	I'd fucking hate getting old, I would. 'I'm
	dreading my old age, dear' [mimicking an
	unsteady voice]. . . . I'd like to go just when
	I'm going off, you know what I mean, when
	the crowd's catching me up, that's when I
	want to go.

Attitudes to women

The masculine style and bravado was at its most chauvinist in relation to women. The culture was overwhelmingly dominated by men, both quantitatively and symbolically. It is difficult to think of it in anything other than a masculine light – though this effect may be compounded by shared patterns of chauvinism between observer and observed. At any rate the approach to women was generally rough, and spiced with a heavy-handed, suggestive humour. Men were the prime movers and arbiters of most things. They set the pace in relations between the sexes. Women were usually accompanied by a man and they did not speak anything like as much as the men. There was a small group of unattached females, but they were allowed no real dignity or identity by the men. They would be spoken to and joked with but in a heavier and more bullying kind of way than with the other girls. They were generally regarded as being 'available' but what basically united them as a group for the men was an imputed inability to attract anyone into a long-term relationship. They tended to be generally less attractive to the boys than the attached girls, although in many ways they conformed more closely to the masculine norms and patterns of interaction.[6]

It was very interesting that all the girls had generally the same tastes as the men. This was surprising because they tended to be much younger than the men, and could not have heard and grown to like the music at the time when it was popular and filled the airwaves. Sue was only about 18 or 19, but had similar tastes to Joe (her boyfriend) who was several years older. Part of the explanation is certainly that there was a recognition of subordination in the way that the girls took over some of the men's important values.

While it was true that girls were dominated, and that there was little tenderness shown towards them, and that sex was treated in a very mechanistic way, there was a form of protection extended towards them. Because of their assumed weakness and lack of real autonomous identity, there was a sense in which the boys would 'look after them' and make sure that they did not come to the harm that they were sometimes jokingly threatened with. To some extent there was a parallel here with their treatment of the dwarf but in the case of women the protection afforded arose from the awareness of an omission: it was the supply of a function women were held to be explicitly incapable of. The dwarf *embodied*, all the better for his lack of imperialism, that function and its associated cultural values. The women had no symbolic place in the world of values in the way that the dwarf did. They were simply the material through which important values worked – 'a man will protect his woman'. This spirit of defence was, of course, a form of affection but oddly enough the affection, if anything, seemed to be warmer towards the dwarf than to any of the women. I

28

never saw a woman's hair ruffled in quite the way in which Joe would end a mock fight sequence with the dwarf.

Two kinds of masculinity

To be quite clear about the nature of this masculine style, it must be stressed that it owed nothing to the conventional notion of the healthy masculine life. Participation in organized sport, for instance, held very little attraction for the motor-bike boys. Their view of the appropriate manly scope of action did not include the wearing of shorts and the obeying of formal rules, nor was athletic ability taken as evidence of masculinity. Attempts to channel their aggressive and robust style into formal sports situations generally met with disaster precisely because it misunderstood the nature of, and the difference between, the two kinds of masculinity. Where individuals did become involved in sport, by and large it was to spoof the whole thing. Rules and conventions were ignored, old sweaters and jeans were often worn instead of neat sports clothing. This was not due, as can so often be thought by the liberal establishment, to material or social deprivation, but to a conscious unwillingness to even begin to be trapped by the paraphernalia, the artificial external definitions of what masculine activities should be like. They would not engage in any safe channelling of aggressive feelings. That would have been dishonest. Masculinity and aggression were mixed in with normal life. To have syphoned these things off in a formal and organized way would have been to deny their identity. A crude, completely unorganized kind of football was played in various situations, in the factory yard, or the patch, or occasionally, in the coffee bar in the club. However, this was completely unstructured, and the boys had total control over the game, so that it could be moulded to their own special needs. A ball against a window, or a ball bouncing around an internal room, gave considerably more pleasure than a well-executed penalty shot.

Nor did the motor-bike boys have much interest in spectator sports. Participation in formal games held little interest for them, and watching such games even less. There were still the rules and regulations, still the narrowed scope of masculine behaviour, still the stereotyped symbols and clothes of the game to disguise fundamental identity, to deny spontaneous expression. An official report[7] notes the lack of interest in sporting programmes when a television set was installed in one of the spare rooms of the club:

> One point of significance that I have noted is the lack of interest in the sporting programmes, which one might have felt, in a strong physical environment, heavily orientated in the male direction, would not have been the case. This is probably because, with our current clientele, the niceties and skills of professional and amateur sport are basically lost, and are therefore unattractive.

This corroborates my view of the masculine style of motor-bike boys. It comments, at a tangent, on the disjunction between the two kinds of masculinity, and then offers an explanation. I should add that the 'niceties and skills' are lost because of the crucial kind of masculine style already articulated among the boys. Their masculinity had a broader sweep than anything contained by the notion of *skill in a game*: the important skills were about preservation of life on a motor-bike, or survival in a fight. 'Niceties' was an alien concept altogether: it managed only to convey something of the distant claustrophobia of middle-class Sunday afternoons and china cups too delicate to handle, too small to satisfy.

Their particular kind of masculinity was easily and often defined by society as delinquency; their 'code of honour' should therefore not be confused with any notion of establishment or conventional honour. Valued tenets of this code – to harden them for a moment in a way that they did *not* – such as impudence before authority, domination of women, humiliation of the weaker, aggression towards the different, would be abhorrent to traditional proponents of honour, and labelled criminal by the agents of social control.

In attempting to understand their life-style, there must be no suggestion of false continuity between the motor-bike boys and wider society; that is, either of falling into a kind of sentimental idealization of their masculine qualities, or of believing these qualities, once translated, as it were, to be positive and acceptable to normal society. These qualities were in fact

The motor-bike boys

consistently regarded as criminal and delinquent by society. No rapprochement would have been possible on either side.

Ethnocentrism and the masculine concrete style

The motor-bike boys frequently spoke of immigrant groups as if they were sub-human. This was a typical view of Asians:

Fred: Fucking dirty black bastards, they're all filthy, you know, you can see 'em on our job [Fred was a scaffolder on a building site] with their fucking teeth all green, and they start yacking to their mates, and looking at you . . . what's they saying about me.

West Indians generally came off only slightly better:

Joe: Anyway, as I said, it's a shame they can't help it, what they are . . . you go past a Jamaican's home, say, with a big party on, the records are nice, the music must send them mad because it sends me mad, they go out in the street and they see a white bird walk past and they go 'Hello, darling' (imitating a Jamaican accent), and that's filthy isn't it . . . we don't do that do we?

Fred: Fucking black bastards, I wouldn't fucking piss on them.

A widespread racialist humour relied precisely on objectification. It dwelt on humiliation and ridicule:

Fred: The black bastards, chuck them all out.
PW: Who are black bastards?
Fred: Every fucking one, the Pakistanis, the Jamaicans, the Indians.
Joe: Our dad used to call them that, you see, and I thought it was the proper name for them. [Laughter.]

Fred: They don't know what the fuck you say to them. I say, 'Bollocks, you black bastard',

31

> they dunno what you mean. . . . Larkin',
> you know, we say, 'You fucking black
> bastard' . . . they dunno what you're saying
> . . . we said to this one, 'You black bastard,
> you cunt' . . . he started talking English
> back to us . . . he never knew. [Laughter.]

Unpleasant as it is, this dehumanization of other racial groups must be understood partly as an extension of the same kind of feeling they had for other out-groups, such as drug-pushers and mods. In all these cases there was the same dismissive derision, the same violent dislike expressed with an incisive abuse. The extra feeling behind their racial attitudes can best be understood by appreciating, again, their special masculine style.

The new racial groups of their urban environment posed a kind of threat to the commonsense establishment of their world. The dark skins, the strange habits, the strange foods, all spoke of a very different way of life, a very different way of understanding life, a very different way of being-in-the-world. Too close a contact, or too imaginative an attempt to understand, may have contaminated them with an importation of some of these strange definitions into their own life-style. This would have undercut some of the solidity of their own world. This is not to attribute to the motor-bike boys any analytic thoughts of this kind – for them it was a simple case of exclusion, of hating. However, if one understands the absolute solidity, the absolute straightforwardness, of the motor-bike world, it is easy to see that a necessary part of their belief system was, so to speak, the denial of any other realities. If there were other kinds of worlds, then theirs might not be the *authentic* one. The solidity of things, which was not simply a belief, but a style and a way of having an incontrovertible identity in the world, might be challenged. Other realities – strange colour, habits and smells – were, of course, extremely worrying bits of evidence, and denial of them took the form of hatred and objectivation of the hated.

This is to say that their racism can be understood in part as a denial of abstraction, in favour of concreteness and 'commonsense'. If the denied abstraction were simply an intellectual belief, it would not have exerted such a threatening force. It was not simply a belief, it was another whole way of seeing things. The admission of other ways of seeing things would have shot from under them not a belief, but a mode of living and being in the world: a mode which utterly relied on the unequivocal concreteness of things.

The strange qualities of coloured people, by threatening security, also threatened masculinity because that security was expressed and maintained in a masculine style. If there were other ways of living, then there were other ways of being masculine. These could be better. The terrible proof of this was the conquest by a black man of a white girl. This kind of fear is particularly clear in Joe's statement about the propensity of Jamaicans to make open sexual advances to white women. This kind of concern is ironic in the light of the particularly rough, and innuendo-laden, approaches that the motor-bike boys themselves made to women. However, it is all the more understandable when one appreciates that, for the motor-bike boys, here was a strange group, full of potential threat, apparently actually challenging them on their own ground, in the terms almost of their own style. That there was any similarity between styles had, of course, to be denied: that would have been to admit Jamaicans into their own world. Instead the Jamaican approach to women was 'disgusting'.

The same concreteness and formal limitedness of their perspectives was evident in their response to politics and current affairs. Attitudes were very clear and simple, and relied usually on the notion of simple action cutting through all the nuances of a situation. This view about the problems of Northern Ireland from Tim is typical:

Tim: I'd just let them get on with it. I wouldn't
     send no British troops there at all. I'd just,
     I'd throw arms to them and let them get on
     with it – wipe all the – I'd give them
     anything they wanted, just let them get on
     with it.

There is no mention of the issues, a very unclear view of who the two sides are and a complete lack of any historical perspective. Again, we have the rejection and denial of other realities.

Rather than attempt to appreciate the causes of strife, they write off different, or disturbing, behaviour as madness. There was a callous indifference to the outcome of this madness – 'Let them fight it out'. It could be callous, because the actors involved had already been symbolically stripped of their human qualities: dead Irishmen were simply abstract bodies toppling over in a crazy game on the edges of the horizon.

Middle-class, intellectual, élitist views of this callousness are unlikely to appreciate its location in a complex, interstructured, consistent world-view. For them Tim's statement may simply be confirming evidence for the omnipresent societal reaction to such as the motor-bike boys: 'they are callous, uneducated thugs.' While admitting Tim's callousness in this instance, and while admitting the general callousness of the group on racial issues, the *general* description cannot be admitted. In other situations, with differing cultural dynamics, they were precisely *not* callous. The callousness we have seen above should be understood as a constituent part of a much larger style of identity and being-in-the-world. The lack of abstraction and the concreteness of things lying at the heart of their identity, and infusing every aspect of the physical and social world, demanded that outside and strange and un-understandable things be treated in a certain manner; this was the only way to maintain the consistent and familiar lines of the local landscape.

One could even argue that this kind of response to outside groups and strange events is healthier than a 'liberal' one. Coming from the other end, much has been written about the dislocating, distorting, disorientating effects of a news medium capable of relaying realistic visual and audible pictures of the most alarming and brutal events from around the world in an instant. If the middle-class liberal is to respond to each of the events in a compassionate, humanist and imaginative way, his feelings would be so ravaged, and relativized, as to destroy any coherent perspective at all. If he protects his vitals and allows a trivialization to deflect the real human potency of what he sees, but maintains a kind of intellectual appreciation of what the issues and human problems are, then he is dissociating his sensibility. It is a kind of schizophrenia to give full intellectual recognition to a human problem, but to deny it full human recognition. This is the kind of bloodless humanism, cerebralized compassion, that in the end can be more insulting, and less humanly relevant, than an apparently offensive spontaneous rejection, which at least springs from a secure human base. Apparently inexplicable comments from some racial groups that, of the two evils, they prefer the full-blooded dislike of prejudice to the synthetic concern of intellectual liberalism, should not be ignored: at least the former respects boundaries. The unintended intellectual colonialism which is often the product of a dissociated humanism can both undervalue cultural formations from the outside, and corrupt them from the inside by the importation of definitions, and dishonest emotion which so structure problems and issues as to render individuals within the 'problem' exactly disorientated with respect to their own cultures. It is also possible to see, from this perspective, that the concerned liberal of the West, tutored by the massive organs of news reporting, and the continuous imperative to 'feel', but only with his head, is often more alienated and less rooted in real human feeling than the groups at which his special dislocated passion is directed.

Pop music and style

The musical taste of the motor-bike boys was highly distinctive and very consistent. They liked the early rock 'n' roll of the 1950s, principally the music of Elvis Presley and Buddy Holly but also that of Chuck Berry, Gene Vincent and Eddie Cochran, and subsequent pop if it conformed to the music of the 'golden age'. They liked the early Beatles music and some Rolling Stones records.

It is difficult to evidence, but the motor-bike boys' fundamental ontological security, style, gesture, speech, rough horseplay – their whole social ambience – seemed to owe something to the confidence and muscular style of early rock 'n' roll. The central role of the music was most clear in the coffee bar of the club. The coffee bar was the hub of the club and the main area of social concourse. It was an extremely large room with cubicled tables and chairs around the sides, pin-tables grouped at one corner, and a juke-box at the front by the coffee bar. To all intents and purposes it was exactly the same as the cafés on the open road. Pop music had always blasted out there in its distinctive way, so that conversation at normal voice levels was often impossible. Of all the cultural elements that went to make up the special atmosphere of the motor-bike café – girls, coffee, smoke, the smell of grease, worn wood, patches of greasy lino, old dirty rugs – pop music was the most significant, and toned all other items with its special feel. It was the music that gave the coffee bar its final stamp of authenticity, as a real motor-bike café, even though it was located at the club. No other club could have matched this distinctive atmosphere. The motor-cycle boys recognized the authenticity of the coffee bar and were quite at home in it. Pop music, anyway, purged it of alien elements: visitors found the full, bustling, and especially the *loud* room slightly unnerving and were glad to get out. But the social behaviour of the motor-bike boys was at its most spontaneous, open and natural in this milieu. For them, the loud, strident tones of the music symbolically held and generated all the important values – movement, noise, confidence. The very air was fuller and more homely to breathe, vibrated by *their* music. Other 'adventures' around the club and local public house always ended up at the central point – the coffee bar. It was the centre of consciousness of the club.

Music also provided the opportunity to dance. The coffee bar was not in any sense a dance hall and at any one time only a small proportion of the people in the room would be dancing. However, dancing was an essential part of the environment, most people would dance at some time during the course of the evening. The girls – especially those without boyfriends – generally danced more, often in groups away from the boys. The normal procedure was for a boy to dance with his particular girlfriend, or for two or more boys to break off girls dancing in the larger mass and dance with them. The dancing was one of several activities. Other groups stood around talking, or playing on the pin-tables without paying any attention to the dancers.

The members did not come primarily to dance, or to 'pick up' girls as at conventional dances. Dancing was simply accepted as a natural part of the whole scene. Joe was a particularly active and well-co-ordinated dancer in the 'bopping' tradition. 'Bopping' is the style of dancing which developed in the early years of pop music, and which has disappeared from current popular practice. It involves much more contact than in more modern dances. The male swings the female around with a flick of his hand or spins her by holding her hand over her head. The beat is followed in an exaggerated way by movements of the head, hands and the whole body. Experienced male dancers also swing round in unison with their partner to arrive back in time to 'catch' the girl as she completes her swing. Although the steps are very simple, the dancing was typically extremely active in the coffee bar with the dancers taking up a lot of room and bouncing around with great enthusiasm. Joe had developed a confident, free, revolving style of his own while expertly controlling the movements of his partner.

Joe describes another – perhaps outrageous – but highly specific and dramatic use of rock 'n' roll records:

> Joe: There's this café, you see, opposite the motel, called the Jubilee, opposite whats-er-name Street, that first street, we used to play a record on the juke-box, a fast record, and we used to drive around the block before it stopped, you know what I mean. The rock 'n' roll used to drive us mad, this rock 'n' roll then . . . used to go around on the bikes. I used to have a rocket then, a road rocket, and used to just get back before it stopped. The time was about, how long was it . . . about two and a half minutes.

As well as the real potential danger to other road-users, this illustrates, again, how the general ambience of the culture could be brought down in a concrete activity to a precise conjunction of its constitutive elements – music, bikes, excitement, disregard, speed and danger.

Private collections of records, which were quite large, consisted entirely of singles or occasionally EPs (extended playing). LPs were not regarded with favour. For instance, Fred dismissed a Chuck Berry record, which otherwise he quite liked, with 'Yeah, but it's only on an LP, it ain't on a single'. Very early 78 r.p.m. singles were seen as especially valuable. The reproduction quality of these 78s was inferior to that of 45s, and the much larger records were of a more brittle substance and more liable to break. Despite this, they were regarded as the 'genuine article' and were always played in preference to more modern reproductions. The concept of stereophonic reproduction was dismissed in derisive terms. It seemed that the very scratchiness and harshness of the reproduction of the 78s, along with their patent bulkiness and shiny, brittle texture, was taken as a clear evidence of their origins in the golden age of music. At any rate, they showed little concern with the technical quality of the music, and tended to be suspicious of technical innovations which threatened to 'mess about with' the integrity of the original articles as they had known and valued them.

Their responses to music were not crude, nor without differentiation. During the taped discussion they expressed opinions which showed a sensitivity to the area and an awareness of the developed and differentiated scope of particular singers. They had an independent sense of the variable relation between the singer and his songs. It was not a case of enthusiasm for one singer that ran through hell and high water: it was certainly not the kind of hero-worship of, or charismatic fixation on, particular pop music stars held to be characteristic of pop fans. Elvis Presley was one of the touchstones for the early rock 'n' roll our group liked, but there was a distinction drawn between the original Presley and the recent Elvis Presley songs:

Joe:	I think he's about the same as Buddy Holly. The old Elvis, the old Elvis is, the new Elvis isn't, you know. . . . Like 'US Mail' is . . . ooh lousy, all that stuff.
PW:	Why?
Joe:	Because it's not as good as the old stuff, is it really? . . . He's probably trying to compete with the pop groups . . . his old style's better.
Others:	Yeah.
PW:	And that's ['You're So Square'] his old style is it?
Joe:	Yeah. 'Jail House Rock' . . . that kind of thing.

Modern groups were not rejected out of hand. Where their

music was close to the early rock 'n' roll they were applauded, but a change of course away from this kind of music was detected very quickly:

Fred: Dave Clark was good when it first came out, 'Bits And Pieces' and 'Glad All Over'. Real rock numbers they was, you had to get up and dance. You had to, didn't you? Then they started making the slow ones, and that's when they dropped out . . . ruddy hell, I could have made that myself. Do you remember, 'Catch Us If You Can'? . . . terrible.

Their feelings about music were so deeply rooted, and so much a part of their commonsense world, that they didn't find it necessary to justify them. Their favourite records were simply enshrined within *the* tradition. Buddy Holly, for instance, was 'a milestone in the history of pop music'. They would no more question the position of such a founding father than they would question their own identity – both were taken for granted in a well-integrated, self-validating, self-explanatory, copper-bottomed reality which left no space for reflection, qualification, or self-effacement:

Yes, very good, I like all his records. I've got all of his records, they're fantastic.

He just never makes a bad record, they're all good.

The songs, well they're perfection.

I never got bored with any of their songs, but these what they do today is getting on my nerves.

Buddy Holly's a perfectionist for a start.

Ooh fantastic, these three of Elvis – fantastic.

Fucking great.

It was, above all, the ability of the older rock 'n' roll music to

39

update itself to changing conditions, to remain deeply relevant, that was valued. Their consistently positive attitude to Buddy Holly and Elvis Presley, although clearly anachronistic, cannot be understood as a nostalgia. 'Rave On', 'Not Fade Away', 'You're So Square' (Buddy Holly), 'Blue Suede Shoes', Heart Break Hotel', 'Hound Dog' (Elvis Presley) were not personal momentoes in a patchworked sentimentality, 'this was a happy day', 'this was a sad one', 'that was my first date'. This is the approach of so many analyses of pop music, treating the songs as ciphers arbitrarily signifying *social* events. These songs were important to the motor-bike boys at *any* stage only because of a special resonance and relevance they had to their *present* lives. The nature of this relationship, put as a question to them, was mysterious. However, they very quickly discerned when a record or a song did not have this quality for them: it had become 'old-fashioned'.

Thus records such as 'Rave On' and 'Blue Suede Shoes' were not hermetically sealed in a period of the past, confined by the interior importance of the individual's emotional biography. Nor were all records after a certain date, after the closing of the seal, disregarded and minimized. Music from the post rock 'n' roll period was accorded value, *in so far as it legitimately embodied and kept alive and gave a style to central contemporary cultural values.* We will look at this more closely in the chapter on pop music.

The use of language

The concreteness and lack of abstraction of the motor-bike boys was clearly evident in their use of language. Opinions were characteristically expressed in concrete images drawn from their experience of everyday life. Here are some of their responses to music they did not like:

Joe: No, it sounds like a load of Irish micks outside a pub on a Sunday, it does you know, with Guinness.

Mick: Well, I think a load of micks would sing better than that.

Joe: I expected him to say 'For the next Irish jig', you know, 'Get your harp out and put your Guinness down' . . . they just sounded like a rabble in a pub playing up, like . . . yes, and a guitar with half the strings missing like – and a cracked old piano.

In a related way many of their basic arguments were *ad hominem*. For instance, where music was disliked, and a vocabulary relating to its immanent qualities was not available, the force of dislike was deflected on to the singer:

PW: Ray Charles, what do you think of him?

Joe: Ray Charles, he can't sing, you know, he's just playing on the fact that he can't see, and I wouldn't want to be blind myself, but that is the only thing selling his records, people feeling sorry for him. He can't sing, it's just playing on the fact that people feel sorry for them, that's what it is, salesmen to sell his records.

Mick: He's just playing on it, though, because he's a wog, isn't he?

Fred: He's an old fucking man, ain't he, he can't dance and he can't fucking sing.

Fred: He's a cunt [Joe Cocker], cut his **hands** off and he couldn't fucking sing . . . them high notes, see the look on his face when he gets the high notes . . . his face goes all over the place, his mouth you know.

Although in the latter case Fred, in fact, admitted that he liked the singing sometimes, the problem was to express what he felt was the special quality of the agonized feelings in Cocker's voice and he plumbs straight for physical characteristics in order to get something of those particular qualities across. Negative opinions were often expressed in terms of action. This response to Ray Charles is typical:

Fred: It fucking bores me to tears. . . . I'd switch
the radio off if I heard that, I fucking would.
I'd turn it on about ten minutes later if I
heard that, see if it's gone.

Opinions generally relied on concrete images for their full
expression. Whenever the argument was abstract, concrete
images were reached for. Here is Mick dealing with the
distribution of scarce resources apropos the Space Race:

Mick: That's 11 Apollos they've sent up . . . the
Russians have sent up 15 . . . that runs into
millions of pounds, all that money on that
. . . millions . . . and just look around . . .
spastics . . . and all that . . . you should put
that right first and then think about going to
other planets . . . you know, they ain't got a
meal, have they, when they get home from
work, half the blokes . . . they can't afford
to have any tea or anything, it's ridiculous.
If they done that first, see everybody were all
right, then go out there . . . when they can
really afford it.

He comes a long way down from 'millions of pounds' to 'tea or
anything'. The essential familiarity and concreteness of the
language is clearest when he talks of having no meal when the
worker 'comes home'. He is drawing – and effectively so – at a
crucial moment in the argument, on personal, concrete,
commonsense images that are a central part of his immediate
world.

Such language should not be rated as inferior to other modes.
It certainly shows a lack of formal education but this is not,
necessarily, a negative characteristic. The point here is to show
not the limitation, but the hardness and substantiality of the
motor-bike boys' language.

There was a consistent and vigorous use of swear-words which
always worked to 'edge up' and dramatize what was said. Far
from being a kind of pollution, swearing was in some ways *the
most successful* aspect of their language use. It held an ability to
fill their verbal range with a force of meaning and muscularity

of style that made for a distinctive and incontrovertible expression of feelings impossible to other, more polite, modes of discourse.

Another way in which their language was concrete was their use of what could be called, even in this context, onomatopoeia. Descriptions were often followed by a simulation of relevant sound:

Tim: Did he die?
Fred: Wouldn't you, if you hit the back of a
            stationary lorry at 70 miles an hour. You
            should have heard the bang – 'baang'. I
            heard it from the other end of the road,
            about 200 yards up the road. He went out
            like a light.

There were frequent attempts to sing parts of songs they particularly liked, or to simulate the sound of an instrument: particularly, for instance, to make the strumming noises of a guitar. There was also an attempt to mimic the voices of particular people they were talking about. This ranged from the 'Hello, darling' of the Jamaican accent, to the shaky old lady's voice of 'I'm dreading me old age, dear'. They were most at ease with language when it was close to life, and most fully part of their concrete masculine style.

4   Shocking styles and conventional politics

The motor-bike boys' attitudes and style were outrageous, shocking and offensive to general society. They also took some satisfaction from this outrage, shock and offence. It would be wrong, however, to read any real political significance into this. They were not in the end challenging the *structures* of society. Indeed, finally, they were, unexpectedly and surprisingly, reproducing them. Furthermore, it is possible to draw a continuity between the bikeboys and what might be called the traditional respectable working class.[8] A profound corollary of their simple, unreflective morality and concrete view of the world was that their spontaneous opposition fell much short of a political critique or attempt to change the larger society.

The conservative and conventional potential of some of their attitudes is obvious. Their belief that women were basically inferior and without autonomous status is an aspect of the common view that the woman's place is in the home with the children and that her field of influence outside should be sharply circumscribed.

Their attitude to drugs, too, was basically conventional. There is the same distrust, the same fear of possible degeneracy that conservative critics have about the drug scene. Their racism also shows their distaste for the different, rejection of the strange, that is held to be common, certainly to the stereotyped view of our tradionally zenophobic working class.

There was also evidence of a surprising conventional 'politeness'. They were particularly critical of West Indians and their 'bad language'. They had their own notion of respectability which can best be understood when placed against wider notions in society of the 'proper':

Joe:	Have you heard their swearin', do you know what their swearin' means? I used to know a Jamaican chap and their swearin' is terrible.
Mick:	Rassclot.
Joe:	Do you know what that means, it's filthy, it's not like when you say 'bastard', it means you ain't got an old man, you know.
Fred:	What's rassclot mean, then? One called me that.
Joe:	I can't tell you . . . it'll embarrass me in front of Sue, in front of everybody.
Tim:	Go on, it won't embarrass us, tell us if Sue goes out.
Joe:	You know what women have – right?
Fred:	A cunt.
Joe:	You know what pussy clot means, you know a tart, if she's, when she's on a period, you know?
Fred:	On the rags are. . . .
Joe:	And the blood clots . . . it's fucking that.
Fred:	Is that right?
Joe:	If they call you a pussyclot, you're a blood

> clot of a tart's doings, you know . . . that's
> fucking filthy, isn't it.

In this way, quite unexpectedly, the motor-bike boys could take offence at something, while they never thought of their own swearing – paradoxically and ironically used even in the course of their expression of dislike – as in bad taste. While their own swearing may have been offensive to conventional society, their dislike of others swearing was not only in line with conventional social values, but self-consciously understood as a breach of wider values – apparently which they subscribed to.

Often apparently radical positions arose only from more deeply held conventional prejudices. A virulent republicanism was based on an even more virulent ethnocentrism:

PW:	How about Prince Charles and the Investiture?
Mick:	Load of rubbish, they ought to have had a Welshman for it, not a bleeding renegade.
Fred:	Yeah, I mean to say, he's fucking Welsh.
Mick:	She's a German, he's a bleeding fall-out from Greece, an exile from Greece, the son's a bleeding renegade and he's made Prince of Wales, it's a load of rubbish, they hadn't ought to be over here.
Fred:	I was gonna say, none of them are fucking English, the bastards, the Prince ain't fucking English, is he?
Mick:	No, no, his old woman's a German, and he's a Greek . . . he can't go back to his own country.

The most striking and important aspect of the covert conformism beneath the brash exterior was in their attitude to work. There was no radical pressure here on society at its most vulnerable point, site of exploitation and class differentiation. From other aspects of their culture it might be assumed that the bikeboys had an indifferent or drop-out attitude to work. The reverse was true. To be out of a job was considered a calamity. Throughout the official report on the club's development[7] the author treats the economic climate of the city as a direct determinant of the number of boys using the club facilities during the daytime. At times of full employment there was so little call for its services that the clubhouse was closed during the day.

This quantitative point presents a minimum proposition about the motor-bike boys' basically conformist attitude to work. On one of the taped discussions Mick got into an argument about work with an outsider called Roger. Roger visited the club to help behind the coffee bar. He was in the style, very loosely, of a 'hippy'. The argument brought out typical attitudes about work, its role and proper organization extremely well among the bikeboys.

Roger:	I'm getting pocket-money. . . . I like working, or . . . my concept of work is probably very far removed from the general, you know.
Mick:	Don't you think this spoils you though, getting pocket-money as you put it?
Roger:	Oh, well I don't get it for nothing, you know, just for existing, you know, it's for other things and that sort of thing, you know. . . .
Mick:	Oh, you work, oh I see.
Roger:	Well, it's not really pocket-money, it's not given for nothing, but it's not a wage, you know.
Roger:	You know it all depends, not what you know, it's who you know, it's all dependent on that now.
Mick:	Well it hasn't been with me, I've had some good jobs, I've been a chargehand. I'm next in line for a foreman up there, and I didn't know none of them before I was there.
Roger:	I mean you can go to a place and you could be qualified in that job and you could do that job better than anybody else, right, but if your immediate superior, you know,

	didn't like you, you can't get on in that place, can you?
Mick:	Well, I can, I mean me and the foreman, we don't get on, but—
Roger:	No, no, I didn't mean you couldn't, I'm just giving an example, this happens all the time, that's why people leave jobs.
Mick:	If a person knows the job and they can do the job without, you know, having to run to the foreman every five minutes, you know, saying you can have a look at this and that, I mean it don't matter whether the foreman or person really dislike theirselves, they've got to get on with the job. . . . You've got a person there who is so-called superior . . . er, yes, so-called because if you've done your work, you've learnt your job and you can do it on your own . . . do it on your own initiative, which you're supposed to be able to do, well then, there's no need for a . . . er, the foreman can be there too, you know, to check on things but apart from that there's no need for it, you know. . . . You've got to have someone . . . to take orders, you know, off the people, and see they get these jobs that they've asked for. . . . You'll get some people, they'll go to work, I mean obviously you got to work a fair day's work for a fair day's pay . . . but you get some people like go there, and they spend about a couple of hours a day in the toilet which is absolutely wrong, so you got to have someone there to chase them type of people.

Everyone's got a superior, you know, you might get just an ordinary foreman come from another factory, and order a job off the bloke who owns the factory, like. We get people who come to our job and order jobs,

47

like, from the gaffer, go and see the gaffer
hisself, and he sees the foreman, he sees us
gives us the jobs, and we get them done. If
anything's wrong, the bloke at the other
firm will give our gaffer a telling-off, and
he'll tell the foreman off, he'll come and tell
us off.

You want a bit of superiority, I mean, I
mean nothing would be done . . . in the
first firm I used to work at . . . er, you used
to get the blokes on the floor that used to
cause all the arguments, the gaffer, you'd
very rarely see the gaffer, you know, but the
blokes on the floor, they might say, specially
in the factories where money is pooled and
worked out, one'll say I'm working a bit
harder than him, why should he get my
share, you know. . . . This is what a
foreman's there for, you know. I mean
obviously you have, like say Roger was at our
place like, and say he's doing well there, if
I've done something wrong, I mean it'd be
no good Roger coming and helping me if he
knew nothing about the job, so it'd be no
good me going and helping Roger if he
done something wrong . . . not knowing
nothing about that type of job. So you've
got to have someone there who knows about
. . . er . . . all the jobs so that person can
see.

This puts Mick and the others in a very much more conventional
light than is suggested by images of them in Teddy boy clothes,
in motor-bike clothes, or in a fight situation or roaring past,
hair-flying, on motor-bikes. It shows the strict limit of any
proper political challenge which they pose for society. There is a
clear attachment to the conventional ideology of working and
paying one's way, so necessary in the working class to the
dominant organization of interests and power. There seems to

be something shameful in Roger's 'pocket-money'. Mick uncritically assumes equality of opportunity and naïvely believes in the value of competition.

This ideology is deeply burned into the commonsense wisdom of the culture. There is a tremendous personal confidence in the way that Mick talks about work. In contrast to Roger, he always turns to the concrete situation and the hardness of his own experience. By and large he sees industry as 'fair' – fair rewards are given for a fair effort – and if skills are mastered, then one can argue a 'fair' case with anyone. There is also a belief in a natural order or hierarchy. He accepts that some people must be in a superior position, half-accepting also that they are personally superior. Work-shy minorities need discipline, and superiors should be respected. The conventionality and strength of this view – and it was a typical view among the boys – is quite surprising when placed against the rest of the motor-bike boys' life-style. The shocking style concealed no impact.

To be clear, the motor-bike boys were not, of course, 'conventional people' and on the whole the wider society rejected them. Their whole culture was offensive to wider society, with its intimidating motor-bikes, extreme appearance and loud music. There was also a general kind of lawlessness, a propensity to fight and steal that was anathema to conventional society. The point is that for all this they did not challenge the main structures of society. For instance, although some of them had personal experience of being in jail, and certainly all of them knew people who had been in jail, they accepted jail as necessary. They largely accepted the values of those who locked them up. They certainly tried to outrage but their offence was basically at a surface level; it was cheek, shock, surprise, disgust, insubordination, insult – never a basic political challenge to institution or belief.

We can partly understand this balance between the conventional and the shocking in relation to their generally concrete forms of perception and secure form of consciousness. Because their world was so straightforward, solid and concrete, and because so many of their attitudes and responses rested on this, they were limited in their ability to imaginatively explore other possibilities for organizing the world. They were delinquent, anti-social and outrageous only within the boundaries set by their immediately apprehended, concrete, world. They had no imaginative faith to live through a gap or a pause to come to a larger perimeter. However, with the horizon thus secured, within that perimeter, they were as challenging as they could be. This is not to put forward a criticism of their cultural style. It is to mark its tragic limits and contradictions.

A post-script

The elements of the motor-bike boys' life-style and its contradictions were clearly demonstrated, though negatively, to me by a small incident. In itself, it had no importance, and I make a completely subjective interpretation. All the same it stuck in the memory as a crucial realization of certain qualities about the motor-bike boys. Fred had been involved in the theft of a motor-bike with Joe. Joe had been to jail before, and was subsequently sent to jail for this. Fred had not been sent to jail before, and although he was not given a jail sentence as it transpired, he did not know at that point whether he would 'be sent down' or not. Although he shared the same bravado and unconcern as Joe in the group context, he appeared to be much less certain within himself. On the night before they went to trial, I saw him standing by himself in the coffee bar apparently half-abstracted in thought. Quite uncharacteristically, he was standing stock still in a slouch, with his hands in his pockets, unaware of his surroundings. Gone were the normal shouts and movement, the normal rumbustious masculine style. He somehow seemed to be in a dead moment, a moment that was not buttressed by unthinking acceptance of reality, or a matter-of-course confidence in identity. For all the world he seemed like a wretched child that had been snatched from home, friends and family, and dumped, lost, in a strange environment that was endlessly threatening. For a moment it seemed, in the face of jail and its un-understandable threat, that he was not sure of who he was, of why things were as they were, or how he came to be placed so specifically at a place and time that had suddenly become so unreal. There was a weakness of the face, and an utter stillness that spoke, in a moment, of the absence of all the things that were usually there. It was literally a moment, for Joe soon came up, and with a sympathetic rough slap on the back jerked him back out of that limbo, back into the obvious world of the motor-bike, women and mates, as much to protect *himself* as to protect Fred. However, it was a brief moment of insight that momentarily laid open, for me at any rate, *by their absence*, a cross-section of the really crucial elements of their life-style and culture.

3 The motor-bike

The motor-bike both reflected and generated many of the central meanings of the bike culture. It must be understood as one of the main elements of its stylistic make-up.

In a general and unspecific way, it was clear that the motor-bike was one of the main interests of the motor-bike boys. Most of their activities were based on this interest. A large part of conversation was devoted to the motor-cycle: discussing new models or comparing performance or describing in detail how repair jobs were done.

The club itself acted as an important clearing-house for spares and accessories, sometimes stolen, sometimes legitimate. The boys regarded the club as a centre of information and supply. On numerous occasions experts were approached by acolytes for detailed descriptions of mechanical repair jobs, or for a 'professional' diagnosis of mechanical problems. A strange rattle or banging, sluggish acceleration, or bad handling characteristics, would send the less knowledgeable enthusiasts running to the acknowledged 'experts'. At *first* sight an unofficial hierarchy *appeared* to be based on this knowledge: individuals with extremely fast motor-bikes, or with recognized diagnostic and mechanical skill, seemed to enjoy a position of high status. A common approach would be to offer the 'expert' a drink or a cigarette as a prelude to asking advice.

Mick was awarded a senior position within the unofficial hierarchy. This was interesting and alerted me to what lay behind the possibly merely random, chance or purely functional technical involvement with the motor-bike. The motor-bike had a specific *cultural* role, and it was its *cultural* meaning which was most related to status in their social system. Mick's mechanical skills were not at an extremely high level, and nor was his motor-bike particularly fast. In his case it was more his *length* of experience and his *type* of experience with bikes. He was older than the rest, had been riding a motor-cycle for longer and, more significantly, had had several accidents. He had been in hospital several times, had broken a number of limbs, and had, as a momento of one of his accidents, a piece of metal in one of his legs holding a weakened bone together. He recounted these experiences with nonchalance and seemed to make no special effort to avoid further accidents – rather he seemed to expect further accidents as a matter of course. Status, then, in the light of Mick's case, was accorded less for technical competence with the motor-bike, than for full citizenship within the *world* of the motor-cycle, for understanding at some level, as it were, not the surface technical details, but the real cultural meaning of the motor-bike: the way in which it reflected important cultural values.

The solidity, responsiveness, inevitableness, the *strength* of the motor-bike matched the concrete, secure nature of the bikeboys' world. It underwrote in a dramatic and important way their belief in the commonsense world of tangible things, and the secureness of personal identity. The roughness and intimidation of the motor-bike, the surprise of its fierce acceleration, the aggressive thumping of the unbaffled exhaust, matches and symbolizes the masculine assertiveness, the rough camaraderie, the muscularity of language, of their style of social interaction.

That sheer technical competence alone was not rated highly is clearly shown by the case of Percy.[2] He had a very advanced technical knowledge of the motor-bike, but was accorded very little status. He did not ride his machine particularly fast, had never had an accident and did not regard the prospect with equanimity. His clothing was within the letter, rather than the spirit, of the motor-bike world. It was simply *too* functional and *too* meticulous to seem natural in this larger symbolic world.

This observation about Percy was important and led to an understanding of the dialectical role of the motor-bike. It mediated not only essential cultural values, but directly developed them in other elements of expressive style. Its nature resonated through the culture. Other cultural atoms took on the structure of its existence, in turn both expressing and further forming the structure of feeling in the culture. The dress of Joe, Fred, Mick and Tim was not primarily a functional exigency of riding a motor-cycle. It was more crucially an extension of the motor-bike into the human zone: this dress was a cultural transposition and *amplification* of the qualities *inherent* within the motor-bike and of the experience of riding it.

For those who have never ridden a motor-cycle, it may not be clear that high-speed riding is an extremely physical experience. At high speeds, the whole body is blown backwards: it was a common way of communicating speed among the boys to say 'I was nearly blown off'. When even a slight bend is taken at high speed, the machine and the driver need to go over at quite an angle in order to compensate the centrifugal force which threatens to throw the rider off, and topple the machine away from the direction of the turn. Novices find this an extremely precarious situation to be in, and can panic. The experienced fast motor-cyclist will not take a complete amateur on the back of the motor-cycle in case a lean in the wrong direction on a fast bend may upset the precise balance, and send them both hurtling towards the tarmac. The experienced driver becomes part of the motor-cycle and intuitively feels the correct balancing at high speeds. If there is anything wrong, it is the fault of the motor-bike.

The dangers and the excitement of bodily wind pressure exist of course for the conventional motor-cyclist, too, but he responds only within a technical (culturally arbitrary) framework. He tries to remove himself from the rawness of the experience. He protects his body, face, eyes and hands from the wind. He tries to close down and minimize the influence within the human of the inherent qualities of the motor-bike. He is, in a sense, contained and sealed by his gear, so that he makes decisions, and controls the motor-cycle, at one remove from the direct experiences which made the control necessary. Thus, he must lean with the machine around corners, and he will feel the force of the wind bodily moving him back, but these senses are both blunted and mediated by protective clothing. The clothing is also pulled in tightly without open flaps, streamlined and smooth to minimize unnecessary drag and wind resistance. Thus, the conventional clothing of Percy consisted of a helmet, goggles, belted waist, tightly closed-in neck, gloves and large woollen socks. The helmet clearly protected against head injury in an accident, the goggles prevented eye irritation from dust or high winds. The belted waist and tightly closed-in neck prevented wind from entering and ballooning the clothes at high speeds. The gloves protected the hands, and, by overlapping the jacket, prevented wind from travelling up the sleeve. Large woollen socks prevented air from pocketing, and kept the feet warm. Thus, in this conventional dress, Percy was tightly packaged in, and given the maximum protection from the inherent dangers and discomforts of the motor-bike. The special characteristics of the motor-bike, its openness to the elements, its instability, its speed, the free rush of air, were minimized as far as possible, so as to render the motor-cycle a neutral form of transport. The whole outfit is a carefully worked out, and carefully put together, attempt to negate the effects and characteristics of the motor-bike: it is the technological answer to the problems technology has created – uniformity, anonymity and featurelessness encircle the rough, roaring, dangerous qualities of the motor-cycle.

The bikeboys' response to the special characteristics of the moving bike is very different. Although their dress contained some of the same basic elements as that of the conventional motor-cyclist, the bikeboys had transformed its meaning and significance by small though crucial changes. To start with, helmets, and goggles and gloves were never worn.[3] They knew quite well that helmets were advisable if only because of a national safety campaign: 'You know it makes sense.' The reason was that helmets and goggles would have inhibited the force of cultural mediation: the *experience* and the *image* of motor-cycling would have been muffled or blocked. These accoutrements destroyed the excitement of the wind rushing into the face and of the loud exhaust beat thumping the ears. The absence of gloves, goggles and helmet means that the equivalent of a high gale-force wind is tearing into the living flesh. Eyes are forced into a slit and water profusely, the mouth is dragged back. The bikeboys allow no disjunction whatsoever between the fact and the experience of speed. Physical consequences are minutely articulated with control decisions of the motor-bike. There is no sense in which the rider is protected by a panoply within which there is calm to make protected decisions about events in the world out there. For the bikeboy, he is in the 'world out there' and copes with handling his motor-bike, at the same time as feeling the full brunt of its movement in the natural physical world.

More generally the motor-bike boy makes no attempt to minimize the drag effect of the wind. Jackets are partly open and are not buttoned down around the throat, belts are not worn. There is nothing to keep the jacket close to the skin, trousers are not tucked away in boots and socks, there is nothing to prevent wind tunnelling to the sleeves. Adornments of the jacket and free-flowing neckties add, although fractionally, to the total drag, an unnecessary drag that would be avoided by conventional motor-cyclists.

The lack of the helmet allowed long hair to blow freely back in the wind, and this, with the studded and ornamented jackets, and the aggressive style of riding gave the motor-bike boys a fearsome look which amplified the wildness, noise, surprise and intimidation of the motor-bike. The point of fast driving was the experience, the expressive force, the public image – never the fact – of speed.

These were some of the dialectical influences of the bike on the appearance and experience of the boys. In the reverse moment of this relation to the motor-bike, they had made physical changes to their machines. They partly changed the objective nature of the bike better to express their own preferred meanings.

Handlebars were often of the large cattle-horn type which required an upright sitting position with hands and arms level with the shoulders. This considerably increases drag, and ironically limits the top speed of the motor-bike. But it improves handling ability and increases the sensation of speed dramatically. The conventional motor-cyclist does exactly the opposite, lowers the handlebars and puts the footrests farther back, so that the body can lie virtually flat along the bike and present the minimum surface for wind resistance. Chromium-plated double exhaust pipes and high exuberant mudguards all helped to give the bikes an exaggerated look of fierce power. It was also common practice to remove the baffles from the silencer box on the exhaust, in order to allow the straight-through thumping of the exhaust gases from the cylinder to carry their explosion directly into the atmosphere. The effect could be startling. The breathy, loud, slightly irregular bang and splutter brought the hardness and power of the metal piston exploding down the metal cylinder, abruptly and inevitably reversing up again, right out into the still air. The minutely engineered turn of the crankshaft brought a power and impersonal ferocity right out into the vulnerable zone of human sensibilities.

An alleyway led up the side of the church to the coffee bar of the club. Members often parked their bikes along this narrow passageway, and stood by them talking, starting and revving their bikes, discussing technical matters or indeed any matters at all. The noise was often overwhelming: the loud thumping of the motor-bike engines seemed to promise sudden movement and action, but none came. Strangers and neophytes could be unnerved by the continually imagined necessity to take evasive action against some fantasy explosion of movement and aggression.

The ensemble of bike, noise, rider, clothes *on the move* gave a formidable expression of identity to the culture and powerfully developed many of its central values.

Perhaps the most massive general dialectical force of the decked-out, souped-up motor-bike on the bike culture and its forms of consciousness was that of death. Death and its mediations and the forms of its subjective and social appropriation were at the heart of the culture. The possibility of accident was recognized – though not sought out – and past accidents were a major topic of conversation. Death on the motor-bike had come to take on a crucial meaning in the culture. It was the ultimate symbolic summing up of courage, masculinity and exhibition.

Joe: I thinks it's the best way. I'll have a bike until I'm about 35, you know. I think it's the best way to die. . . . I'd like to go quickly, mind you, out like a light, 'bang' . . . fast, like, about 100 miles an hour . . . hit a car . . . smash straight into something.

PW: What are the chances do you think of having

	a serious accident?
Joe:	Oh well, I'm a nut case, you know, on a motor-bike, it might do. I've had some near misses, you know, through crash barriers, and I've had concussion and things like that without a crash helmet.
PW:	But did that make you think?
Joe:	No, funnily enough it didn't, everybody else said 'I bet that's made you think'. . . . You see, that's why I think I may die on a motor-bike.
Fred:	I'd like to die on . . . I'd like to die on a bike, that's the way I wanna go, fucking great, I'd hate to get old.
PW:	Why?
Tim:	The thing is—
Fred:	Hang on, you daft cunt.
Tim:	I'd like to.
Fred:	It would be a great sensation to croak out on a bike. . . . I'd like a fucking smash, got to be a good one, or I don't want to go.

Certainly the death rate from motor-bike accidents at the club was appalling. This is from the official report on the club concerning the period summer 1967:[4]

This period has brought a number of major disasters to club members, both in terms of personal injuries and death on the roads. Four deaths were recorded in August alone, and each brought with it a major shock to the organization with feelings of hopelessness and despair. . . . Funerals were attended by large numbers of members wearing ordinary clothes [motor-cycling gear, etc.] and pall bearers were provided from friends.

Death on the motor-cycle had its effects not only on consciousness, however, but on the material organization of the club, which in its turn, of course, further developed particular kinds of meanings and values within the culture. On the altar table in the church[5] was a large embossed book lying open all the time with the names and dates of the death of past members of the club who had been killed on the road. The pages were turned daily to record exact anniversaries. It was one of the familiar sights around the club to see, alone, or in groups, past girlfriends, friends, acquaintances or admirers of a particular victim looking at the book in solemn ritual silence.

Normally the motor-bike boys treated the church with complete disregard. Before the discussions Joe, Mick and others would often play with a large medicine ball, throwing it back and forth to each other down the length of the church, crashing it through the chairs and bouncing it up on to the altar. This does not imply sacrilege. They simply treated the church as any other building. However, when a member of the club was killed in a motor-cycle crash, there was always a very well-attended memorial service in the church and a formal entering of his name in the memorial book. In these particular moments of crisis the motor-bike boys turned towards the church not out of a sense of religion, but out of marking what they regarded as an important event with formal recognition. Death on the motor-bike sought out a ritualized, formal expression for itself in the face of countervailing everyday attitudes. The motor-bike boys did not have their own institution for recognizing an event of such extreme importance. The church, its paraphernalia and rituals, were turned to because they offered for creative appropriation and modification ready-made and widely recognized *formal* ways of according significance. It was at the memorial church service that the rider was well and truly recognized as dead, and could stay dead, and was marked as such in the memorial book: a kind of formal root for the dark glory, the collective mythology of the motor-bike culture. It did not matter that the church rituals were not understood – they could not have been understood in the way the church would have wanted them understood and they were anyway filled up from the outside with new meaning. What mattered was the sense of presence, the sense of order, the sense of marking within time of a crucial event. Thus, at these times, there was very special conjunction of a traditional received form and a modern informal form. The motor-bike boys who in so many other circumstances delighted in the outrage of conventional society, at a certain point within the internal expressive life of their culture – at a point which was both crisis and transcendence – turned in an act of cultural fusion to a traditional institution to borrow its solemnity and ritual. This regard for death, the fascination in its rituals, the need to push beyond the normal bounds of their culture for these rituals, attest the degree to which death on the motor-cycle and danger on the motor-cycle were integral to the whole culture and locked in, expressed and developed many of its meanings.

The apocalyptic death on the motor-bike and promethean inflation of the victim was registered in another dialectical adoption and adaption of an unlikely form chosen for its inherent power to express significance. It was said that deaths on motor-cycles were always reported in the local press, whereas deaths on scooters or in motor-cars were not reported:

Fred: They publish a remembrance in the paper,
      you can cut it out, like, and put it in a
      scrapbook. They always do that when you
      croak out on a bike, they always put it in the
      paper, you know, no scooters, motor-bikes,
      Johnny Gibson and all them lot, all fucking
      in the paper.
Joe: Johnny Gibson, that was my mate, I talked
      to him, you know.

Again, we see a surprising conjunction with, and use of, conventional society. An element of conventional society was able to mark or accord significance to something of importance within the culture, in a form which was possible in no other way. No internal cultural form could give the public visibility and substantiality which the motor-bike death required. Newspaper items were cut out and kept, and widely talked about, both at the time and afterwards. Past figures, and the manner of their death, were one of the main topics of conversation among the boys. Individuals, who in their time often had achieved no particular status, soon become heroic, mythological subjects of the bike culture folk-lore. The build-up of a pantheon of figures in this way owed much of its legitimacy and resonance to a creative borrowing and decontextualizing of elements of the conventional news media and established church.

Essentially, then, the motor-cycle was not limited to a functional use within the motor-bike culture. It was taken up, not blocked, by experience. It was allowed to make a full dialectical register on human culture. Mechanical qualities were recognized, appreciated, extended and transformed into human qualities which then pushed through for their own material recognition, instituting yet further circuits of development. This is not to posit a cybernetic model of the relationship between experience and technology where machines condition and over-ride specifically human qualities. It is the opposite. It shows a form of man's domination of the machine. The motor-cycle has to be controlled, the direct physical consequences of riding accepted, before the 'spirit' of the motor-bike can be appropriated and anthropomorphized. The bike plays its part not in some other constructed, but in a *humanly* constructed, world of meaning.

The motor-bike was not, therefore, simply one object in a random collection of objects and activities that occupy the life-space of an underprivileged group. External notions of 'culture' might attach no more importance to it than the table or chair we sit on – a functional object totally lacking in 'culture'. In fact there can be a tight, dialectical formation of meanings and attitudes around apparently functional objects in the normal course of living. Such a distinctive and meaningful construction, such a developed *expressive* function, based on a form of modern technology, cannot be assumed to be valueless and devoid of *cultural* meaning. It is increasingly *the form* of cultural life, *everyday* life, for underprivileged groups.

4 The golden age

You know this type of music, all this loud stuff, you know, it
sort of gus with leather-jacketed kids, you know. . . . You
might not have heard a record before, and you come down
here and hear it, and like it, but – it's still in you that type of
music, because if you've got a likings, it's there isn't it?

Mick

Pop music was a manifest and ever-present part of the
environment of the motor-bike boys: it pervaded their whole
culture. In simple quantitative terms, there was a massive
interaction with pop music. It is clear, however, that the
significance of this relationship went very much further than an
arbitrary or random juxtaposition.

The motor-bike boys had very specific tastes that were not
part of the current pop music scene, and were not catered for in
the on-going mass-media sources. They liked the music of the
early rock 'n' roll period between 1955 and 1960. By current
standards in the commercial market and the pop music
provided by mass-media channels their tastes were at least ten
years out of date. By deliberate choice, then, and not by the
accident of a passive reception, they chose this music. This alerts
us to the dialectical capacity which early rock 'n' roll had to
reflect, resonate and return something of real value to the
motor-bike boys.

Their preferred music, especially that of Buddy Holly and
Elvis Presley, was part of the first really authentic and integrated
period of rock 'n' roll. It marked the first distinctive break
between the record as an artefact and the sheet music it was
based on. Because these singers brought together a number of
elements, first made available by the initial pop opening

62

explosion, unified them in a unique way and combined this with a distinctive personal style, it was virtually impossible that another artist could repeat the performance simply from the sheet music. For the first time the single record really came into its own, and the stylistic integrity of the singer made *hearing* the record more important than seeing the musical score. Buddy Holly's distinctive style lay mainly in the restless, exclamatory, alert quality of his voice. There was no mournful submission to fate but an active confrontation with life and an awareness of the possibility of change: 'You say you're gonna leave . . . but that'll be the day when I die.' Elvis Presley's distinctive treatment of the songs relied on the easy riding of the urgency in the rhythm from the bass and the guitar. His voice was close, personal and confiding though always ready to take a defiant stand on his own cultural identity: 'Get off my blue suede shoes.' This historic period of rock 'n' roll came to an end with the death of Buddy Holly in an air crash in February 1959: an event which sealed the authenticity of the *genre*: early rock 'n' roll.

The bikeboys' musical preferences, therefore, were *objectively* based on the identification of fundamental elements of the musical style. The music did have a distinctiveness, a unity of construction, a special and consistent use of techniques, a freshness and conviction of personal delivery, a sense of the 'golden', 'once and for all' age, which could parallel, hold and develop the security, authenticity and masculinity of the bike culture.

The social nature of this general consonance of structure was apparent in their comments about music. A need for security and authenticity, the lack of relativity and concreteness in their life-style was almost literally *seen in* the qualities of their preferred music. Early Elvis Presley and Buddy Holly were changeless and secure; 78s were preferred to singles; original versions of songs were preferred to repeat versions. The masters of the golden age were absolutely unchallengeable:

Joe: Yes, after all this time, people are still recording him. Mick Berry tries to take him off, and Bobby Vee and Tommy Roe, they've all had a bash at taking him off, so it

must be good . . . there's more in his fan
club now than there ever was. . . . I do
though he's got more fans than he's ever
had now . . . and they're still releasing
tracks of his LPs, and that's still after ten
years. . . .

Fred: Any rock 'n' roll singer that's worth his
weight in song, like, has always recorded
some of Buddy Holly's . . . you go all
through the top groups, they've all recorded
one or two . . . always, every group, so there
he must be liked by even modern singers,
mustn't he? . . . 'True Love Ways' by Peter
and Gordon.

To dignify this sense of 'the tradition' with a platonic parallel
would be foreign to the boys' own expression, but it may help
in illuminating the essential status of the valued originals. One
could regard these originals as ideal creations: holding the
ultimate in musical value in their ontological genuineness.
Records that were repeats, or similar in form and style, were just
shadows cast on later years. Records owing nothing to the
originals were meaningless and were ignored. They did not even
have the reflection of authenticity played across them. They
were without identity. Thus, even though a repeat record may
be preferred in its immediate impact, it could never replace or
seriously challenge the original. Records in altogether different
styles were not responded to for their own qualities – they were
dismissed at a deeper level. The originals had a value which was
beyond demonstrable qualities, and could therefore never be
challenged by demonstrable qualities.

The motor-bike boys' preference for 78s over 45s can be
understood in this light. Although their technical quality was
demonstrably inferior to the more recent 45s, they had a bulk, a
brittleness, a distinctive tactile presence that all spoke of
genuine origins in the golden age. The scratchiness of the
reproduction, far from detracting from this total effect – as it
would for a neutral observer – enhanced the 'soul' of the song
for them simply because it was over-riding evidence of the
music's authentic origins.

With a grounding of their life-style in ontological security, the motor-bike boys expected their music to have a similar integrity. There was not a field for the free play of choice in music, as there was not a field for a free play of feeling about reality. The music, in one sense, had to be the only possible music, and secure within its own distinctive style. Veneration for the golden era implied a location of personality and group identity, in just the way that the physical world did – the same demands of genuineness could be made upon it.

It is in the light of the 'golden age' and its cultural resonance for the motor-bike boys that we can understand their attitudes to later artists. The Beatles' albums *Revolver* and *Rubber Soul* and *Sergeant Pepper* were immensely successful records, but they had clearly deserted the spirit of early rock 'n' roll. With their melodic asymmetry and complexity of rhythm, they had an authenticity of their own, but it was not the authenticity of the 'big beat', rock 'n' roll era. These records did not have the intrinsic capacity to return anything of significance to the motor-bike boys. They were in fact disliked, they were considered 'daft'. However, for a brief period after *Sergeant Pepper*, on singles at any rate, the Beatles returned to a simpler, more intense vocal style, based on the work of much earlier singers. 'Lady Madonna' was reminiscent of Fats Domino's styling, and 'Get Back' of Chuck Berry's. For the motor-bike boys these were the last flowerings of the Beatles' genuine rock 'n' roll personality. They were greatly appreciated, but everything after (except for some of the records from the Plastic Ono Band who deliberately returned to earlier styles) was despised.

The Rolling Stones, too, whom the boys consistently rated highly, can be seen as giving a rebirth in the 1960s to the rock 'n' roll of the mid-1950s. The Stones' music began with strong simple rhythms and conventional chord patterns and metre taken fairly directly from Chicago rhythm and blues. The vocal style was that of black singers such as Chuck Berry, Muddy Waters, Bo Diddley and Howlin Wolf. The only influence from a white singer was, in fact, from Buddy Holly. There was experimentation, often accidentally, but it was always – apart from a brief digression in *Her Satanic Majesty Requests* – from a hard rock base. The Rolling Stones were most successful with numbers of their own composition, such as 'Satisfaction', 'Get Off My Cloud' and '19th Nervous Breakdown', because these more accurately reflected the English cultural situation, but musically they remained consistent with the atmosphere and spirit of the original rhythm and blues sources. Although Mick Jagger's copying of Negro speech rhythms sometimes seemed inauthentic, his consistent alignment with early rhythm and blues and the successful adaptation of rhythm and blues to the English setting without loss of its essential spirit, completely outweighed this factor for the motor-bike boys. Bascially Mick Jagger was, if not an original, at least an inheritor of hard rock. He held the internal codes. In this he answered their need for authenticity, security in identity, and straightforward belief in a fixed-centred universe.

Early rock 'n' roll bore authentic potential meaning for the motor-bike boys in another important way – the powerful *social* meaning with which it was historically invested. Early rock 'n' roll was seized upon by the young in the mid-1950s in America and England as their very own music. It was mainly theirs because it so clearly was not their parents'. Early rock 'n' roll films were associated with rioting, fighting and seat-slashing in the cinemas. The new 'dancing' was violently active compared with any of its predecessors and the 'live' performance of the stars (particularly Elvis Presley) was openly sexual in a way that only American Negroes had been held to be capable of before. Parents and established society could not condone such open subversion of traditional values. The dissociation of one group is the association of another. A large-scale distinctive musical *genre* became, perhaps for the first time, truly available to the young. This was the beginning, the first distinctive awakening, of what we refer to generically as youth culture. It was crucial for the motor-bike boys that this take-over, this social furnacing of an expressive form, was characterized – aided and abetted by lurid media treatment of particular incidents – by violence, aggression and anti-social feeling. Rock 'n' roll, then, came to the motor-bike boys rich in absorbed, highly appropriate social meanings. This 'double fit' of the music – its *prior* social imbuement and its particular *objective* structure – explains much of the motor-bike boys' attachment to the music.

Not only was the motor-bike culture about security of consciousness and authenticity, it was also about the linked expression of these things in movement, in style, in physicality, in 'handling yourself'.

One of the most noticeable things about the music they liked was the prominence of its *beat*. It is music for dancing to, for moving to, and clearly has the ability to reflect, resonate and develop in a particular way a life-style based on confidence and movement. Elvis Presley was consistently best in his fast-moving beat songs. With his gyrating hips, outflung arms and coy angling of the head, he altogether did away with the image of the stationary singer. Almost every early record cover shows him *moving* and, of course, his stage name will always be Elvis *the Pelvis*. Buddy Holly's style, too, relied on a strident beat, and the alert quality of his voice was enhanced and projected by the clear beat. For the period and for his colour (white) he was very strongly influenced by black rhythm and blues music: this is one of the reasons why he was the only white singer seriously to influence Mick Jagger. The driving, dancing rhythm of more traditional rhythm and blues comes through in his records time and again. Sometimes, as in 'Not Fade Away', the music is virtually taken over by beat and rhythm, with the melody totally subjugated to a transfixing rhythm pattern. The Beatles, as we have seen, in their early days played a kind of up-dated rock 'n' roll, which again relied on a fundamental 'big beat'.

The progress of the Beatles could be described simply in terms of the loss of this big beat. They became more sophisticated, using melodic asymmetry and complex rhythm patterns. The latter music became very much harder to dance to, especially in the concrete, direct, bopping-to-the-rhythm dance patterns of the early rock era – a style of dancing which had none of the 'freaky' free-form movements that later styles developed to match the asymmetry of progressive music. The motor-bike boys ranked the early Beatles very highly. They became progressively cooler about the later Beatles. They despised some of their late 'really stupid stuff'. To simplify, the process of the bikeboys' disillusionment was commensurate with the disappearance of the big beat from the Beatles. The Rolling Stones, much more consistently than the Beatles, kept to the strong, simple beat of rhythm and blues. Of all post-early-rock-music, the Stones have kept closest to the elemental function of pop – providing music to dance to. Mick Jagger, in performance, with his outlandish talent for movement, mime and gesture, personified in action the movement-potential of his music.

Their preferred music, therefore, was clearly answerable to the restless movement of the bikeboys' lives. Musical discrimination was based essentially on the displaced category of social and physical movement. The musical quality they universally disliked was slowness and dreariness. The quality they prized was fastness and clarity of beat. This is from a discussion of Ray Charles:

PW: Say a bit more.
Joe: Just what I said when I heard it before, it's too slow and dreary, isn't it . . . eh? I like music that makes you get up and do something, like.
Tim: You put the Beatles against them and you know straightaway, don't you, or the Stones, you get the Stones or the Beatles with them, they're outclassed, ain't they? You can't understand a word he says . . . and the beat, well, there ain't one, is there?

The antidote to boredom was always movement and their preferred music not only reflected this, but provided a concrete, formative outlet. A good strong beat was the prerequisite for dancing. As Joe said: 'That's all you need.' The importance of being able to dance to music was stressed time and again – and as an internally coded aspect of the music unaffected by particular contexts such as the immediate desire to dance:

Joe: Oh, I do like ['Lipstick On Your Collar'], one of the best girl singers out . . . she [Connie Francis] warn't as good as Buddy Holly, but she was one of the best girl singers out.
PW: Was there anything else about that particular record?

Joe: Oh, yes, you can bop to it, any record I can
                        bop to, I like, that's it.

To praise a record for its relevance to dance was not,
therefore, to say that it was actually always danced to, or that it
could only be appreciated when dancing. It was meant as a
description of a general quality of the music that was quite as
evident whether actually dancing or not. Again, a section from
the discussion of Ray Charles:

Mick: If people go to a dance, you know to enjoy
                        themselves . . . they don't want to listen to
                        stuff like that . . . you can't get up and
                        dance . . . you'd just sit there moping all
                        night . . . I'd walk out, I would.

The literal meaning of the song lyrics was not often
considered. At one level they were taken for granted so that
appropriate words and meanings could always be read in: the
possible range of meaning was very limited so that the bikeboys
always knew, and took for granted, the kind of things that were
said. Lyrics became important only negatively, when they
obtruded, broke expectations or were not understandable.

In relation to the importance of style and movement in the
culture and of the selection and generation of representations of
these things, we can understand a further dimension of the
bikeboys' exclusive preference for singles. Singles were
specifically responsive to the active, moving listener. They only
lasted for 2½ minutes. If a particular record was disliked, at
least it only lasted for a short time. It could also be rejected from
the turntable more quickly without the difficulty of having to
pick the needle up to miss tracks. Exact selection could also be
made so that the order of records was totally determined by
individual choice. To play an LP was to be committed – unless
you were prepared to go to a great deal of trouble – to someone
else's ordering of the music. By and large, LPs are more popular
with an audience which is prepared to sit and listen for a
considerable period, and with a certain extension of trust so that
unknown material can be appreciated and evaluated. LPs are a
cheap way (as distinct from singles) of building up a large
collection of songs within particular traditions. Often there will

be tracks on an LP which have never been very popular, but which are of interest to the expert, or the devotee or the technician. LPs tend to serve the interest more of the 'serious' listener, who is concerned to appreciate all the aspects of a particular field, and not simply those to which he is already attracted. Of late, LPs have also been produced which have been conceived as a unit, parallel in a way to the opera or extended musical piece. Dating from approximately *Sergeant Pepper* by the Beatles, the so-called progressive groups particularly have been concerned to produce LPs which are imaginatively conceived as a whole in this way and which are meant to be taken as a whole at one sitting. All this implies an audience which is stationary, sitting, not engaged in other activities and prepared to devote a substantial length of time to the appreciation of the music alone. Of course, there are many exceptions to all this. An LP, *Elvis's Golden Hits*, for instance, is specially produced as a cheap collection of Elvis's singles. The attraction is specifically that of a cheap package of popular singles. However, generally, and especially in contrast to singles, it holds true that the LP audience is stationary and mono-channelled towards the music.

This kind of situation is clearly completely inappropriate to the motor-bike boys. The connotations of the LP form were quite contrary to the fundamental elements of their life-style. They are usually moving, engaged in other activities, responsive to music only when it is not boring, and most interested where music responds to their particular mood. Their preference for singles was so overwhelming, indeed, that, quite apart from inherent musical qualities, the absence of a single version of a song was held as *prima facie* evidence of its inferiority, and even well-liked songs were passed over if the LP version only was available. This might be taken as clottish, obstinate inflexibility, until it is realized that, in fact, the experience of listening to the same track on an LP (as on a single) would not have been so enjoyable for the motor-bike boys: it would not have been the same experience precisely because they would have felt a lack of control, an implied seriousness, an unresponsiveness, which would have inhibited the free flow of response. Their preference for singles was simply an honest, logical projection of a coherent set of attitudes on to an appropriate object – not the random obstinacy of the unimaginative.

The assertive masculinity of the motor-bike boys also found an answering structure in their preferred music. Elvis Presley's records were full of aggression. Though the focus was often unspecified and enigmatic, the charge of feeling was strong. In the atmosphere of the music, in the words, in the articulation of the words, in his personal image, was a deep implication that here was a man not to be pushed around. His whole presence demanded that he should be given respect, though, by conventional standards, the grounds for that respect were disreputable and anti-social. Buddy Holly's music was not so aggressive, but it was utterly secure in its own style: it insisted that its range and interests were important and deserving of recognition. The Rolling Stones' music and image has remained entirely 'unrespectable' in its opposition to the adult world, and its espousal of hooliganism and permissiveness. Their 1960s music especially was harsh and angry – striking cruel or sardonic poses. The violence of the vocal delivery invested the lyrics with meaning far beyond the power of the cold words. There was also, in the Stones' music, an assumed superiority over women, and a denial to them of personal authenticity, which was very close to the attitudes of the boys themselves. The Beatles were not aggressive in such an outright fashion, and did not symbolize hooliganism in the same way, but there was a vigorous release of feeling, and an utter confidence in their style of playing, which gave the music considerable power and muscular control. In some ways the Beatles' early songs were a celebration of youth: they expressed a naïve male ethic of control in an alienated world. All this made the music particularly responsive to the special confidence and rumbustious, masculine movement basic to the bikeboys' cultural style.

The motor-bike boys preferred music, then, that clearly resonated and developed the particular interests and qualities of the boys' life-style. The music had an integrity of form and atmosphere as well as an immediate, informal, concrete confidence. It belonged to the golden age of pop as well as maintaining an immediate responsiveness to living concerns. This dual capacity to answer to the basic ontology, as well as to the surface style, of the bike culture, explains the centrality of the music to the culture.

This centrality of rock 'n' roll music is surprising in one sense. In view of the limited power of the motor-bike boys to change the internal form of their music, it might be expected that the dialectical power of the music in the culture was limited. They *selected* as between types of music, of course, and the fantastic precision and distinctive type of their taste attest to the degree to which *selection* from what exists can be an important ingredient of cultural development. In the reverse moment, of course, the music itself had exerted an immense influence on the culture and its material practices, which in their turn further modified the culture, and forms, ultimately, of appropriating the music – all within a complex unity.

We have looked at the obvious connection between rock music and dancing. There also seemed to be a direct connection between rock music and fast bike-riding. Fast riding was incited by the feel of the rhythm in the head. And in reverse all the qualities of fast dangerous riding, movement and masculinity seemed to be summed up in – were part of – similar qualities in the music. As we have seen, stylistic, assertive masculinity was a generalized quality of the culture as a whole. It owed much to the articulation of feeling between the bike and pop music. There were several, half-explained, sometimes obscure statements concerning what seemed to be an experiential synthesis between rock music and riding the motor-bike:

Tim: It helps, like, the sound of the engine . . . try and get a beat in my head, and get the beat in my blood, and get on my bike and go.

Fred: If I heard a record, a real good record, I just fucking wack it open, you know, I just want to wack it open.

Tim: You can hear the beat in your head, don't you . . . you go with the beat, don't you.

Tim:
I usually find myself doing this all of a sudden (moving up and down) with my feet, tapping on the gear or something stupid like that.

Tim:
Once you get the beat in your head, you really go, you start going.

Fred:
Yes, the beat of the motor-bike, the beat in your head, you want to beat the traffic . . .The more the engine roars, the more I have to give it, and I think, 'You bastards.'

Joe:
Once I've heard a record, I can't get it off my mind, walking or on the bus, humming it, or singing it, you know. I think that's in your head . . . you know . . . if you were on a motor-bike, it'd drive you mad that would, it's all in my head, you're bombing down the road.

Interestingly, where dancing as an immediate corollary and physical expression of the music was stretched to the full, or unavailable, then riding took over as an extension of the same mood and feeling. In an important sense that mood or feeling would have remained basically suppressed or undeveloped were it not for the cycle: music – dancing – riding – music:

Joe:
If you hear a fast record you've got to get up and do something, I think. If you can't dance any more, or if the dance is over, you've just got to go for a burn-up.

In a more violent way fighting can be seen as an extension of emotion along the same dimension. In a telling comment Joe said to Fred, 'He can't dance, you see, I get up and dance, he gets up and hits.' Fighting for Fred had an integral relationship with pop in the sense that it was a playing out of emotion embodied by the music – it would not have happened without the music. Though we must condemn this, mark it as one of the final limits of the culture, and recognize here the reproduction of a traditional regressive, self-entrapping, working-class trait, we must also recognize the distorted and displaced fashion in which it marks a distinctive sense of bursting through a block: of communicating *something* deeply. Remember that aggression, 'handling yourself', movement, masculine bravado and courage were important values in the bike culture. Fighting, fired and furnaced by a primitive rhythm, was a powerful expression of those qualities in the moment that it marked their tragic, self-destructive limits:

Joe: If the dance is over, you've just got to go for a burn-up.

Fred: That's like me, we were at the Alhambra dance and whenever a good record came on with a big beat I had to get up and hit some fucker, or do sommat. It did, it sent me fucking wild . . . it just sends me mad. I'll tell you one thing that used to send me fucking mad, that was 'Revolution', 'Revolution', any rock anyone with a big beat in it, the fucking sound, I go fucking wild, I do. Me and Pete, you know, we got banned from a dance, and the police came practically every week because we used to fight every week, couldn't help it, it used to send us wild. There'd be a perfect stranger and Pete would go and punch his head in, he wouldn't get back up, only 'cause the records, certain records, they'd send us fucking mad, they would, they're old beat records. . . . If I hear a good record it . . . fucking, you know, I go in a temper, it just puts me in a temper if I'm just there, so I have to thrash out, it sends me wild, that fucking 'Revolution' used to get me mad.

Fred: I dunno, but it sends me fucking mad, but

	. . . all the big fast ones do. I have to bang my feet or do something, I can't help it. Have you ever been in a dance and you get that tensed up over the record, you feel like fucking lashing out on everything and everybody there?
PW:	Well, I just have a pint and keep it in.
Fred:	No, I don't drink, you do it the easy way, you can do it the other way, you can go and get pissed down the road and come back there to it, and then listen to the record.
PW:	How about the bike?
Joe:	Yes, give it holy stick down the road . . . fucked up, I get like that, sometimes I fucking shiver with a record like that. . . . You get that tensed up, you know, you just let it . . . get it all out, you know, then your bike, or fighting somebody, takes the heat off you, doesn't it.

Drinking alcohol would be an 'easy way out', it would not recognize the link between emotion and music. A *full* response, spilled over into action and real-life movement. There was an integral connection which it was as dishonest to break as it was reprehensible to keep.

The capacity of the music to influence the culture of the bikeboys, on the one hand, and the exact and searching selection of music made by the boys, on the other, allowed a real, though limited, dialectic of experience with its own form of material practice to function in their culture. It brought about very clear basic homologies between the social group and its music. We should respect and learn from this creative, cultural achievement in an area normally thought of as 'culture-less', deprived and manipulated.

A post-script

A really adequate account of the internal parameters of the bikeboys' preferred music and its specific ability to hold and retain particular social meanings must be more technically rigorous than this chapter has been. Musicology is the discipline which has the formal resources for this task. It is possible to outline a framework for such an analysis.

Fundamentally, rock 'n' roll has opened up 'new' possibilities because it has avoided being trapped by the received conventions concerning rhythm, tonality and melody.

Most importantly rock 'n' roll escaped from the determinations of the classic bar structure simply by giving equal emphasis to all the beats of the bar. This subverts the bar form, and actually replaces it with a continuous 'pulse' or basic primitive, standardized rhythm. This regular beat, rather than melody or harmony, is the basic organizing structure of the music. Its constancy and continuity mean that the music is, so to speak, a steady stream, rather than a varied structure. The structure of classical music, with its hierarchy of beats in the bar, meant that it existed clearly in a time sequence – some things had to come before others. In subverting the discontinuities of the bar, rock 'n' roll also subverted the sense of order and of ordered time – if all the elements of a piece are the same, it does not matter in which order they appear. Rock 'n' roll music can be stopped or started at any time; it can be turned back or forward; it can be suspended here and carried on over there; it can be interrupted; it does not need an emotional decrescendo with which to finish. One of the most characteristic features of Buddy Holly's singing style is his 'hiccup' an interruption and confusion of tone that would never be tolerated in classical music. Elvis Presley's 'Jail House Rock' comes to an abrupt stop and then starts again. One of the commonest end-piece forms is the fade, the diminution of a constant beat into nothing – an impossible concept for any previous musical forms and, incidentally, one that relies completely on modern technical methods.

The tonal aspects of rock 'n' roll are also interesting and innovatory. The music was not caught up in the end of the possibilities of harmony in the way that classical romantic music was – resulting finally in atonality and polytonality because it never seriously took them up. Rhythm replaces harmony as the basic organizing principle of the music. The normal rules of progression, and forms of cadence, are replaced in rock 'n' roll by a kind of anarchy and the creative exploration of the possibilities of new electronic equipment: electronic 'spacing' techniques which anyway eclipse harmony; exploitation of fluidity of the recorded as against the formalism of written music; echo chambers.

By avoiding conventional tonality, the music can also avoid the great emotional structures of crescendo and decrescendo which are the essential characteristics of classical romantic music. In conjunction with the bar, chord progressions fix conventional music in a time sequence – at the very least the decrescendo has to come after the crescendo. The disregard for tonality in rock 'n' roll further enables it to experiment with repetition and 'timelessness' – in a sense to experiment with the 'space', the 'here and now', instead of the ordered time dimension of music.

The melodic element in rock 'n' roll is generally unimportant. There is little conventional chord progression and very limited development of linear expression in the form of a tune. Where they exist, melodic pieces are short, repeated several times over, and frequently totally obscured by rhythm. The suppression, break up or non-existence of the melody means that each part of the music can be understood by itself. For its appreciation the music does not need to be taken as a whole, as in the classic bourgeois aesthetic principle. It also means that from the melodic, as well as rhythmic, point of view, the music can be suspended or broken off at any point, or faded at any point. The tonal and melodic features of the music, therefore, add to the 'pulse' effect created by the constant rhythm beat.

If the main lines of this argument are valid, what is the relationship of this internal structure to the culture and style of the motor-bike boys? Most crucially this music allows the return of the body in music, and encourages the development of a culture based on movement and confidence in movement. The classical European tradition has steadily forced the body and dancing out of music, and made it progressively unavailable to the masses, and progressively harder to dance to. The absolute ascendancy of the beat in rock 'n' roll firmly establishes the ascendancy of the body over the mind – it reflects the motor-bike boys' culture very closely. The eclipse of tonality and melody in the music is also the eclipse of abstraction in the bike culture.

Second, and in a related way, the suppression of structured time in the music, its ability to stop, start and be faded, matches the motor-bike boys' restless concrete life-style. As we have seen, it is no accident that the boys preferred singles, nor is it an accident that the rock 'n' roll form is the most suited to singles and its modern technology (fading, etc.). Both the music and its 'singles' form are supremely relevant to the style of the bike culture. For the boys, music has to accompany not determine, it has to respond in the realm of their immediate activity, not in a separate realm with its own timing and logic which require acts of entering into.

In one way, and concentrating on its oppositional aspects, the whole motor-bike culture was an attempt to stop or subvert bourgeois, industrial, capitalist notions of time – the basic, experiential discipline its members faced in the work they still took so seriously. The culture did not attempt to impute causalities or logical progression to things. It was about living and experiencing in a concrete, essentially timeless, world – certainly timeless in the sense of refusing to accept ordered, rational sequences. Hearing the steady strum of the motor-bike exhaust (reminiscent of the 'pulse' of their music) riding nowhere in particular (as in Joe's dream) is a steady state of being, not a purposive, time-bound action towards a functional end. In a curious way, death on the motor-bike stopped time altogether: it fixed and secured this symbolic state for ever. In sum, they were exploring a state, a space, rather than a linear logic. The stream-like quality of rock 'n' roll matched, reflected and fitted in with this concern. It could be stopped, or broken off or easily changed (as with the single) and did not intrude, with its own discipline, into concrete and spontaneous activity. As the music suppressed the discontinuities of the bar structure, it also suppressed ordered, rational time. The stream 'pulse' quality of the music could be taken and used as timelessness – or certainly as an escape from bourgeois time. In this sense, there was a profound inner connection with a life-style that was so utterly concerned with concrete action in the present and the immediate secure experiencing of the world.

Rock 'n' Roll = beat

↓

able to dance music

Part two

Not very much of humanity contemplates itself. Humanity is in a pretty horrible state . . . You know, if you try to change your consciousness, if you try to modify it and look, you'll run away. The fact of looking is an important thing.

Les, 1970

5 The hippies

1 The approach

I made contact with 'the hippy scene' of a large industrial city in November 1969. 'Head' is a more recent title for the 'hippy', more exactly representing the later drug experiences of the culture, and derived from the more specific 'acid head'. I will use both terms in my account even though 'head' is really more appropriate to what I shall be describing. 'Hippy' is maintained basically because it is the term by which this cultural phenomenon is still generally known.

My initial visits comprised of hanging around a public house called the Anchor, which was the main focus of the hippy community at that time. I observed the general situation and chatted to the barman about the different groups and personalities. I asked him who were the central, long-term characters on the scene. I introduced myself to various groups and explained my interest in their life-style, culture and music as frankly as possible. This period was difficult in that, in contrast to how I had contacted the motor-bike boys, I had no institutional avenue of approach. Of course, in comparison to other groups, the hippies were fairly approachable and were always willing to talk to 'strangers', but in other ways the hippies were more forbidding than other groups, because of their disarming propensity to question motive and social front.

I asked three distinctive groupings of people occupying slightly different positions on the scene if I could visit them at their 'pads' and tape discussions about their musical tastes and general attitudes. For a period of five months I spent some time each week, moving generally around the pubs and meeting places and recording several discussion sessions with the different groups. The typical pattern of these meetings was for us to listen to various types of music and then lead on to a general discussion from their responses to the music.

These three groups spanned a fair cross-section of the whole scene. Les, Val, Stuart and Mary were placed centrally, both in the sense of their social contacts and in the classical 'hippiness' of their style. Paul, Tony and Roger shaded off towards the 'drop-out, down and out' end of the hippy cultural spectrum. Keith, John and Bob shaded off towards the more conventional end of the spectrum. The age-range in all the groups was from late teens to late 20s. Of all the individuals, only John and Bob were working. They ran a small business in the neighbourhood. Of the others, some had dropped out from full-time further education, some had dropped out of technical and skilled jobs, some had dropped out of the lower managerial range of industry and commerce.

A typical day for me during the research would begin with a dinner-time drink in the Anchor, followed by an afternoon in a flat, or an afternoon with one or another of them doing a specific job. My car was particularly useful since there were not many cars around and individuals were very glad of a lift when they had something specific to do. For instance, in the early period of the research, I drove Les into the city centre one afternoon, to get an electrical component for his home-built stereo record-player, and I drove Stuart to the Social Security offices on two occasions. During these times, I came to know the individuals very much better, and I would to some extent 'be with them' for the rest of the day. Evenings would see a return to the Anchor and a fairly lengthy drinking session with a much larger group in the main bar. The loose sub-groupings tended to dissolve during the course of an evening at the Anchor, and there would be very fluid movement within the much larger group. Very often I would arrive with a group or an individual at the pub, and be separated immediately and not see them, apart from brief passing contacts, until closing time.

After the usual long session in the pub with its great range of contacts and movement, relatively distinct sub-groups would again emerge, and go off to different 'pads' to continue the night. I would accompany one of 'my' groups, usually the Stuart/Les group. We would stay in the 'pad' talking, playing records and, if it was available, smoking cannabis, until two, three, or four o'clock in the morning. It was in this final period of the day that I sometimes suggested that I might play some of my own records and tape responses to different kinds of music. By and large, the taped sessions fitted in well, since listening to records and talking is precisely what they *would have been doing* anyway. Discussions took off entirely without any prompting, and the tape-recorder was virtually forgotten.

Though I was not taken as a hippy, nor tried to pretend, I was allowed into the general social circle, particularly under the patronage of Les. I spent long periods in different people's 'pads' and in the pubs which were known as hippy meeting-places. The following is based on my general observations of the scene, participant observation, soaking up of the general hippy ambience, casual talk, directed talk and various taped group discussions.

2   The hippy identity

The hippies did not live in a world of personal certainty and had a far from certain grip on their own identities. Where in the 'straight' world this is a cause for concern, for the hippies it was a source of richness and the base for expanded awareness. In a crucial sense the hippies were operating with an abstraction of 'normality' strung out above the lidless eye of their own self-consciousness. Consciousness, and awareness of consciousness capsized a belief in the everyday self. Fundamentally, they could never believe the world to be real, but they were in no sense *doomed* to this fate, they welcomed it as a profound insight. Instead of being *locked* in their inner selves, which is often the consequence of the conventional loss of reality, they *discovered* their own consciousness. In this sense, then, a state of ontological insecurity was welcomed as liberation, and not feared as disease: it set the mind free from that micro-dot of consciousness called 'normality'.

Spirituality

The hippies were massively concerned with the possibility of

85

transcendence and with fuller states of awareness. This fuller awareness could never be realized, it lay permanently as a goal on the horizon. On the other hand, it could never be admitted that this goal was impossible or illusory.

A central paradox to be explained if we wish to understand the hippies is this: how could the notion of something beyond be kept alive when it could never actually be possessed? Their resolution of this paradox took the form of the playing out of an interminable and symbolic game.[1] The result of the game always promised to bring final proof of transcendence, and the ambience of this result came back through the game so that one could be forever on the brink of experiencing ultimate truth.

As long as the game could be *meaningfully complexified*, the scent of success remains in the air, the senses remain tensely expectant. The *game forever holds the possibility of resolution*, the starkness of failure need never be faced: existentially the game is a solution. I will not do *artificially* to extend the game because that is a recognition that the prospect of success is not real. Nevertheless, there must always be a move left, another change to see dimly what *better play* would gloriously bring.

All their widely differing accounts of spiritual experience had one thing in common. This was a fundamental sense of the oneness of things, the belief that all contradictions were resolved, all opposites reduced, all consciousness joined, in an over-arching super-awareness. At the heart of this spiritual monism was a realization that one was God:

Norman:	That's I think one of the most blissful moments if you want to . . . the knowledge that you're God.
Val:	You may just come into contact with yourself, you may find just your own ego, but something really deep inside you says to you, you know, that you have found God.
Les:	On acid it's the most incredible moment in your life that if ever you get the void, what they call the void, the bright light, the understanding of the pure energy state, when you get to that and you've

realized, on acid, and you think, 'Yes
that's the pure energy state', and when
you've finished tripping and you think
that again, it freaks you right out of your
head.

Although monism described a goal for consciousness, this
goal could never be reached and permanently inhabited. It was
forever hovering just out of grasp, none the less real for its
ever-retreating nature. It promised what ecstasy would be like,
if only the mind's reach were greater. Their notion of spiritual
fulfilment stood on the ambiguous and shifting line between
the unprovably transcendent and the significant, promising,
but still secular experience. For their spirituality to have been
nearer the transcendent would have resulted in disbelief – if
ecstasy were known, then what were its terms and grammar? Why
could it not be described? For it to have been nearer, the
secular would have resulted in disinterest and spiritual
slackening. Both of these results would have constituted a failed
end-game, and the feeling of spiritual excitation would have
been lost. The ever-receding, but ever-promising, aspect of
their spirituality is particularly well brought out in the following
extract:

Norman: If the whole thing was one pure blissful
           state, everybody would be going fucking
           mad, they would be doing their own thing.
Les: If you're saying it's a pure blissful state,
           you are making a statement of fact, not of
           consequence, and that is a blissful state.
Stuart: No, he is not saying it is a blissful state.
Les: He said it.
Stuart: If it was, if it was –
Les: If it was a blissful state, it's blissful, no
           matter what you want to say afterwards,
           it's blissful, man, and if the knowledge of
           good and bad is blissful, that's one thing,
           without a knowledge of good and bad that
           could be blissful. But the point is, it's
           blissful.

87

Stuart:	We're only saying if there was nothing to compare, if there was no comparison for anything.
Norman:	People always want a comparison.
Les:	Bliss, do you live in bliss, in your life total bliss now?
Stuart:	Is it hell, man.
Les:	How can you say what the important values are?
Stuart:	Because the nearer you get to bliss –
Norman:	Because I've experienced bliss.
Les:	Do you know where bliss is?
Norman:	I've experienced bliss for myself.
Les:	Perpetual bliss?
Norman:	Well, it wasn't perpetual but it was long enough –
Les:	You can't say, then?
Val:	You can't understand the concept, then.
Norman:	I can because I was glad to get out of it.
Les:	Well it can't be fucking bliss, man.

Les:	But when you didn't want to stop in it, it didn't become bliss, it became something less than bliss.
Stuart:	You didn't enjoy coming in or coming out.
Les:	Partial bliss, yes . . . momentarily.
Val:	Well, did you want to stop like it?
Les:	I wished I knew how to stop in it you know, but I came out of it, 'cos I got paranoid.
Val:	Well, that's it.
Les:	Yeah.
Val:	You got paranoid.
Les:	But that's the point, I didn't know how to stay in it, you know, if I could know how to stay in it, I would stay in it.
Val:	Well, you're looking for a way to stay in the experience?
Les:	Yeah.

Val:	So, therefore, you're not capable of stopping in it?
Les:	*Yeah, but the point is that I would like to be in that experience.*
Val:	Well, that –
Norman:	You've got a point there, Val, because no matter how you get into an experience of bliss.
Les:	Yeah –
Norman:	It just proves that we weren't meant to stay in it.
Val:	The human mind cannot conceive it –
Les:	It does not – it does not prove it at all.
Val:	Eternity. . . .
PW:	Can you say what bliss is?
Norman:	You can't because as soon as you talk about it, you destroy it.
Les:	It's total ecstasy, bliss is.

Two apparently contradictory feelings I had during the early stages of the research were resolved by the realization of this dimension of head culture. On the one hand, I was impatient: the hippies seemed to be going around in circles and refusing to come to a concrete perspective on anything. On the other hand, I felt a great deal of uncertainty and confusion. This ranged from a feeling of general social gaucherie to subjective unease: a feeling of being submerged by something it was impossible to define.

In fact the hippies were covering a lot of the same ground, and rejigging familiar elements in various combinations. But my impatience lessened when I understood the purpose of it as being, at some level, the attempt to reconcile a too trivial reality with a grander notion of spiritual destiny. To make the point in a more sweeping way – it was a *cultural living out* of a version of the 'middle state of man'. The *living out* of an idea was in its own way heroic. It was fuller, more resonant and honest than its dry, cerebral statement.

On the other hand, my unease before their culture was justified. It was a kind of insight into the essentially bottomless and contradictory nature of the hippy solution. You *could* be engulfed, existentially, in the interminable attempt to know the unknowable. Only by forever just putting off the ultimate, could the hippies believe in the ultimate. This *was*, for those not committed to it, a frightening paradox.

Subjective experience

The hippies insisted on the importance of subjective experience and of the 'now'. The past always had disappointments and the future threatened with 'objectives', and 'plans' which might discredit their belief in something beyond – 'If it's there, why not plan for it?' the tyrannical future might ask. A commitment to 'plans' must never be allowed, because the failure of plans would deny that their *object* had ever been valid. The 'now' was all-important, and carried in it the maximum spiritual suggestiveness: it could be felt, but there was no time for disproof. Like a fountain of water supporting a ball, the present could continually buoy up, continually save, their awareness from falling to the prosaic. The experienced stream of time could forever forestall a recognition of collapsed inspiration. There were ever more moments coming to save the failure of this one. Past or future did not have the same sense of being 'in media res'. Past or future could not buoy up spirituality with the excitement of the ever new. In the past or future there was time to answer questions, and these answers might produce a final closing of spiritual ambition. At least the hinted answers of the present, the precarious promise of the moment, kept all the possibilities of consciousness open.

The capacity to savour – for joy or pain – immediate experience and to exclude thoughts of past and present, thoughts of planning, came paradoxically from a sensed loss in personal autonomy.[2] It came from a cultural recognition of the lopsided dialectic between external determination and experience, between the weight of history and individual action. The hippies were released from the chains of the protestant ethic – strangely through a more advanced sense of the inevitable. Instead of the careful reign on desire; instead of the careful chalking up of good deeds against a never-known acceptability in heaven; instead of iron discipline mobilized to block evidence of damnation, the hippy freely accepted 'damnation'. He never had had a chance and there was no point in fighting. The mind could relax from guilty self-vigilance, it could be used instead to savour what was there through no fault of its own. The hippy was released from the tyranny of hoping himself better than he was: he accepted, went to meet, the 'worst' in himself. He had every expectation of enjoying it. He was free when he knew he was determined.

This depiction of the emphasis on immediate experience may seem to contradict what was said earlier about the insecurity of identity among the heads. If their extreme self-consciousness was set over against the commonsense world, if they did not believe it, how come they were so minutely interested in it? In fact, of course, it is only the detached mind which finds the everyday world problematic or worthy of minute interest. The normal, incorporated consciousness takes everyday events, and the present, for granted: planning for the future in the light of the past keeps its real attention. The present is nothing more than what connects the past and future: it enacts the plan. The hippy has frozen this logic, scrapped the critical path of conventional time, and held the moment for itself. He is forever in an exotic land, even when most at home.

There were many examples of the interpretation of common scenes in a special light:

Les: You walk into a church, and you can see other . . . you can see other people's communications all around you. Go look at the stonework and some guy fashioned that for you, you look at the windows and some artist designed those stained-glass windows for you and you're communicating with that artist, and those craftsmen, and then you have the stillness of the church . . . you have the contemplation. . . . Just the surroundings which have been made for me . . . this moment in time.

There was a recurrent fear expressed in various forms, and structuring the culture itself, that modern society was progressively challenging, or making impossible, the unique response, the authentic experience. *Technological rationalism* might extend life but it was at the expense of its quality. Humans were in danger of becoming unfeeling, sterilized packages of flesh:

PW: This smoking report from the Royal
            College of Physicians?

Stuart: They're more than likely right, but it ain't
            gonna stop me smoking.

Les: I'd like to see a veterinary report on a
            cow's smoking.

PW: What do you mean?

Les: I mean, you know, it just about carries as
            much weight morally.

Stuart: They'd stick you in a flaming plastic bag,
            that's always my argument, they'd stick
            you in a plastic bag . . . and wash the air,
            and make sure you eat perfect food, you'll
            live a lot longer, man . . . they'll ban
            smoking, and then the next thing they'll
            ban is perhaps boozing and then perhaps
            they'll ban you crossing a road, you'll have
            to go underneath or over it.

Materialism, rationality, and a mechanical ordering of existence was, for the hippy, systematically destroying man's ability to experience: to enjoy the immediate fascinating environment:

Tony: You take a coach-load of factory workers to
            the seaside, and they get out, you know . . .
            and they say, 'Ah, it's fucking cold', and
            they get back into the coach, off to the
            nearest pub, and they get pissed, and they
            get a few crates in, and they go home, and
            they say 'We went to the seaside and this
            pub, and that pub, and', but they didn't
            stand in the sea, just looked at it, you
            know, and maybe threw a few bits of bread
            to the gulls, man . . . they can't see it, you
            know . . . it's too cold for them, or the
            wind's blowing sand into their fucking

                sandwiches or something . . . I think it's a
                shame.

It was commonly said that 'Europe was worked out now'.
You had to 'get to the East, if you want anything real'. They
blamed the ratio-technical order for the complete
impoverishment of human sensibilities. Authenticity,
directness, honesty were now only to be found in odd pockets of
Western society – among the poor, the rejected, the
stigmatized – where the damning liberation of rationalism and
materialism had not yet reached.

Identification with underprivileged groups is a much noted
characteristic of the hippy movement, most clearly represented,
of course, by the espousal of the American Indians by the San
Franciscan hippies. The basis of this interest and identification
was not simply curiosity, nor the desire to be different and
colourful, nor a romantic association with the outsider and his
style. The aim was to feed on dense experience: to be with the
smell of real human bodies before the dehumanizing
juggernaut of material society squashed out the real human
juices. Oppressed cultures were used as a set of forms, a milieu,
within which to express their criticism of the ratio-technical
order and what *it* suppressed or no longer had. In no real sense
did the hippies become Indians or poor blacks, or prostitutes or
tramps – or only in a guilty disingenuous sense – but they found
their own significance in what they took groups to be: a
significance to be understood against the dominant society and
with respect to their own special awareness:

Les: Frank Zappa said, 'That most people look
                and see society reflected in its face. I prefer
                to look up its arse-hole'. . . . He just wants
                to see the arse-hole . . . its garbage cans,
                things that it rejects, people like divorcees,
                people like prostitutes, people like
                psychotics, any misfit. . . . That's where I
                like to be at, you know, sure, I mean we're
                at its arse-hole, man. When people say,
                'Look, dirty filthy hippies', you know, I
                think what a fucking gas. . . . Society's

pretty rotten, and you see rotten people in
society like the hippies, the skinheads and
youth, or spades, or any rejected
sub-culture. . . . Yeah . . . and there are
some really beautiful cats among them, with
really beautiful heads, and society's
hell-bent on stopping them communicating
because of its own paranoia.

Powerless omniscience

Among the hippies there was the sense of an immense knowing.
Their feeling that the conventional world was quite unreal fed
this particularly strongly. They felt that they had penetrated the
tricks and appearances that most people took for reality. If they
could never quite reach or deliver the profound truths beneath
this surface, at least they had travelled out of the mists of
normal consciousness. This sense of omniscience was, if in no
other way, socially supported by mutual affirmations of
superiority:

Stuart: It's about time somebody took some notice
of the ideals we've got, and people like us.
The ones we have got are better than the
ones they've got. We've tried asking, we've
tried pleading, we've tried every way.

Val: We're heads, you know, we're heads, we
know what we are, we're not kind of . . .
we're not people who need discipline, we
don't need any form of discipline at all, but
there are people who do need it.

But there was always a sense that they were doomed never to
be listened to, or if listened to, like Cassandra, never to be
believed. They were in a 'catch 22' situation. When they had
been in the 'real' world, in the days when they had a job and a
conventional life-style, they had had some leverage: people
would listen. But then they had nothing to say. With the
rejection of conventional life came elevation and omniscience,
but *also* a receding influence over conventional others. The
passage and its outward signs destroyed their credibility for

those left behind. So the heads felt doomed to know, but never
to be believed. Powerlessly they watched the 'real' world go by
with a private knowing. As they knew it better, they were less of
it:

Paul:	What gets me so mad is that they're so happy with the way that they're living.
Roger:	That's because they don't know any other way.
Paul:	You try to tell them that they're not happy, and I guarantee you will get a fist between your teeth, and it's happened.
Tony:	They just call you a communist.
Paul:	Yes, they do, they say, 'You're a communist, a dirty-looking pig, get out.'
Tony:	They [society] give you these things like TV to brainwash you, and keep you happy, while they're really going to town on you . . . you try to persuade any one about that . . . phew . . . you know.

3   The style of identity

This hippy identity was enacted in a mannered, exaggerated,
expressive style. Style for its own sake, it seemed to outsiders,
with hyperbolic flourishes beyond check or control. Despite the
extremes and garnishes, though, the style held a certain
mystique, an inner logic that did not yield itself to the casual
observer, or enthusiastic imitation.

Appearance

Despite the apparent articulacy of the heads, their verbal power
was not aimed at the expression of any truth about themselves.
Expression was more an elegant fashioning of what was
assumed. Words were a delicate tracing on the surface of their
innermost meanings. The most *direct* expression of their nature
was in their appearance and bodily movement.

  The long hair of the hippy was a central expression of his

identity. First, and most important, it was a potent assertion of freedom—especially in relation to conventional society:

Robin: If you ask me why I have my hair long, I'd say, principally because I like it . . . and to kick society in the bollocks . . . wave my fingers at them. . . . Hair's important to me in as much as it's part of me, you know, at the moment I want to have long hair because I think it looks nice, and for no other reason, but at the same time, I'm not going to cut it off just because somebody that wants to employ me, wants me to have it off before he'll employ me.

Second, hair was a symbol of natural processes and of an organic and natural form of society. As the juggernaut of technological materialism had squashed all the humanity out of an older, richer society, so it had processed the individual into an unfeeling robot. One of the important elements in this robotization was seen to be the systematic removal of non-functional natural characteristics, most crucially the removal of personal hair – the clearest and freest and most expressive of natural human symbols. Long hair for the hippies symbolized a return to nature, and a desire for a denser, more experiential, more harmonized, more organic form of communal existence:

Norman: It's natural, it grows, it's there, you know, it's not that I'm making it grow myself, it's there.
Roger: It's fuck all, but I like it. Why should I, you, have to get something cut, something which grows naturally on your body, to get an unnatural job. . . . I thought Jesus had long hair, and a lot of people liked him.

Third, long hair demonstrated affinity, and identification, with underprivileged groups. I was told more than once that the hippy's long hair was the equivalent of the black man's skin. When I pointed out the unavoidable nature of skin colour, it did nothing to destroy their belief in the connection. Long hair, beards and facial hair were the stigmata of their cultural election. They felt that there *must be* some automatic and inevitable *external* manifestation of their internal life. Had their hair been cut off, their election would have reappeared and marked them out in some other compulsive form. Long hair was *experienced* as part of them.

Of course, their long hair was not simply a *natural* expression. It was not entirely appropriate to natural activities or to work, for instance. It had gone beyond that, it had been taken to the 'freaky', to the 'outrageous'. This was typical of the use of themes and styles of naturalness in the hippy culture. They had their own surreal version of naturalness through manners, cerebralism, psychedelia and super self-consciousness. A riotous, abstractly mechanized, gorgeously clumsy enactment of the 'natural' was right at the centre of their style. This is not to minimize their interest in, and affinity with, nature, but to guard against too organic or too romanticized a view of the hippy attachment to it.

Clothes were another important expressive item in the bricolage of the hippy style. At the individual level each individual concocted his/her own very personal expression, but what united the hippies was more interesting than what distinguished them from each other. There were some common denominators of style. All their clothes seemed to be permanently out of joint with the immediate environmental determinations of their situation. They were functionally inappropriate. The twentieth-century, utilitarian basis of clothing had been flooded over with incoherent symbols which denied or mocked its logic. It was not that another base was suggested. It was not one fashion competing with another. The symbols were too confused, contradictory and imprecise for this. It was the internal disorganization of *fashion*. Their clothing was – as with so many aspects of their style – a colourful unseating of conventional wisdom. It was the visual dimension of a many-faceted game with an unsuspecting stiff and pompous partner. It was the dynamic and play of the style in context which carried the point – not a dry, consistent content. Symbols of opulence existed alongside symbols of poverty everywhere in their clothing. Particularly rich items of clothing were soiled or dirty, or creased to deny their role in any consistent class notion of dress. Poor materials, colourless shirts, threadbare jeans, denim jackets or waistcoats were thoroughly washed and cleaned to deny their associations with poverty. Bare feet braved the coldest days, but great sheepskin coats, heavy cloaks and ankle-length cardigans were worn on the hottest days. Functional items of clothing were worn for their expressivity: elaborate items of clothing were worn for the most prosaic functions.

The same sense of functionalism being disorientated by a chaos of symbols was evident in the hippy 'pad'. Signs of the necessities of living was very obvious. Bread, jam pots, unwashed cups, knives, spoons, rolled bags of sugar, brown stained teapots lay all round. If you felt hungry, you simply got up and spread some jam on bread. Eventually someone would be persuaded to make a cup of tea. But in among these things were old posters, records, scattered clothes, poetry quotations written in large letters and hung on the walls, brightly coloured underground newspapers, tins of tobacco, packets of cigarette papers and masses of wires, amplifiers, decks and speakers. Rooms were flooded with objects, untidy in one sense, but more importantly, intensely homely, personal and chaotically meaningful. The 'pad' was not simply a functional place to live in: it did not have the clinical tidiness of the middle-class home, the devotion to use. 'Use' was gently mocked by the randomness and lack of logic of the plethora of objects, and by their different and contradictory associations.

The unapproachability of many hippy 'pads' was also a kind of denial of functional reality. They were typically on the top floors of multi-occupied houses, and though front doors were festooned with masses of bells, none of them seemed to remotely connect with the inside. Of course, this difficulty of communication was a useful thing to keep the drug squad at bay, or at least to delay their entry, but it also seemed to be appropriate in a symbolic sense. It separated them from the real and commonsense world: their *private* world was guarded by a difficult approach that only the chosen knew how to negotiate. Straights made themselves immediately available to any kind of visitor: they laid their privacy open to any casual call. The heads guarded their privacy, protected the non-utility and chaotic expressivity of their pads from heathen misinterpretation.

The body was also used as an expressive instrument by the hippies. Unlike the motor-bike boys, they seemed uncertain in their bodily movements. They did not have the unconscious co-ordination of those who take their bodies for granted.

Reality, for them, was in the head, though the body was a useful carrier for its picture show. The body was a fiction it was better to believe in. It was an expressive piece which could be dressed and carved to express your meanings.

The body itself had no life. But the lifelessness of the hippy body was not the 'sickness', or odd-angled wet dejection, that conventional society often sees it to be. It was, in its own right, a culturally developed and meaningful expression. The distinctive 'coolness' of the hippy was partly in this ability to use the body as a metaphor – the clumsiness could not easily be imitated. The bad co-ordinations spoke of a kind of stance before existence, an unspoken understanding of the nature of 'reality' and one's own position in the dialectic of determinateness and freedom. The lifelessness of the body was not the helplessness of illness but the suppression of bodily expressed values which were too enthusiastic, too obvious, too straightforward, too positive, too *centred* and *active* to be 'hip'. Clumsiness and lifelessness of bodily style was a recognition of special position, an anti-style that separated their knowing and developed consciousness from the smooth gaucherie of the conventionally 'healthy'.

Interaction

The hippies created a mode of living with one another which was carefully pitched and special. The timing, patterning and movement of particular situations were vastly more important than particular 'objectives' in particular spaces of time. There was no frank and commonly understood meeting of minds. Their interaction was a delicate tracing on what was *assumed* between people – the fundamental unreality of life, the game, the knowing, the desperate importance of the 'now'. To verbalize the unsaid was to be a neophyte. To be unaware of the unsaid was to be 'straight'.

And through all the social interaction was a gentle mockery of conventional modes of being. The carelessness, the openness, the androgynousness, the oddness of their actions, all highlighted the *pomp* and *self-seriousness* of the 'straights'. The 'straights' could not penetrate appearances. They played out a cosmic joke *seriously*. They were like adolescents in a spiritual puberty, adopting the grave manners which they took to be those of maturity.

But their collective behaviour was not all sport: an impish game around the marble feet of society. Though they apparently had all the time in the world, there was a kind of desperation. A gripping of the present could equate the future with calamity. There was always an impending sense of crisis. In a sense their interaction was the continually played out last act before the void, before engulfing consciousness extinguished the self. So the style and elaborate processing of action was charged with extra importance. It was enjoyable and mannered for its own sake, but it was also a courageous act of defiance against the seriousness of the fate that seemed imminent. It was the spinning of a fine mesh of support to hold you up from the void of your own self-awareness.

One of the most noticeable elements of this complex style of interaction, conventionally registered, was sheer contrariness and unreliability. Against the backcloth of their mockery of 'straight' values, and their earnest spiritual introversion, the first conventional virtues to be jettisoned were punctuality and reliability. The church workers in the field noticed this continuously. They experienced many disappointments and let downs. Here is the local vicar:

> Another thing I've found, too, is that people have come to me in the Anchor and said 'Can I come around and see you?' and you've got appointments set up for them and everything else and you stay in for them and they never arrive. This has happened on quite a number of occasions, which means if they want to see you, well, you go down and see them. . . . You wonder in the end whether to take any of them seriously, or just to say yes, and put your tongue in your cheek . . . but you can't, you know, you can't be too cynical, otherwise you start being unchristian and stop showing love.

I was 'let down' several times. People arranged to meet me

and then completely forgot about the arrangements. The future was not really believed in, so almost anything could be promised for tomorrow. On the other hand, if they were interested in you or in what was happening, they would stay, no matter what other arrangements were broken, until the thing was worked through. There was none of 'I must dash now' or 'I can only stop a minute' which prevents a real meeting so often in conventional society.

Within the contrariness of the hippies' complex social style was, however, a central insistence on personal authenticity. They expected people to express themselves directly rather than through the role they occupied:

Stuart: You can take a society like this one . . . come in to the Anchor. . . . You can get a guy out of work, never worked in his flaming life, talking with a guy earning £5,000, or £6,000 a year, and it doesn't make the slightest bit of difference. . . . That's where you get the freedom around here, a hell of a lot, is the fact that people will accept people as people rather than what their social status is. Around here you don't give a damn whether a guy's got a million quid in the bank, or million quid in debt, you know I'd accept him as him. Now if he's a bum, you don't have to like him, but that works both ways, a rich bum or poor bum, you just don't like the guy if you don't like him. If you like him, you like him, not what he's got, whereas a lot of 'straights' keep up with the Joneses.

Authenticity for them was not the demand for a spartan *reduction* of personality. The demand was for the expression of a unique *self*. Extremity and flamboyance of style were positively welcomed as the expression of the particular of the special. Most 'heads' were 'real characters'.

Being a 'real character' meant, in part, understanding the importance of the *big gesture*. There was a hippy wedding during the period of my research which involved the bridegroom in some classic *big gestures*. Long before closing time in the Anchor, where celebrations were taking place after the wedding, the barman told me, passing by, that he had no idea how he was going to get the bar shut. When closing time did come, his protestations had no effect whatsoever. The publican became concerned and eventually threatened with the law. Eventually it was the bridegroom, not the publican nor the police, who decisively called closing time and emptied the pub. He did this with a big gesture. Standing on a table, he carefully donned his long velvet cloak, put his hands together in a diving position, and called out, 'Will anyone catch me and take me outside?' People cheered and shouted as he launched off the table in to the arms of the people below. He was carried out triumphantly. The pub was emptied in seconds. There was quite a mêlée outside on the pavement and the bridegroom kept things going with another gesture. The pub was on a slip road off a main road. Cars were slowly edging past. Quite spontaneously the bridegroom leapt on to the moving bonnet of a well-polished Rolls-Royce. The driver was surprised, but did not make an issue of it. There were about 50 'weirdos' around who seemed to find it particularly amusing and who might do anything if he acted wrongly. He drove forward gently until he was clear of the main crowd and then stopped, gratefully, to put his passenger down. Two or three people tried it, shoppers stopped in the street, soon there was a large crowd: it had become an urban spectacle. The culmination came fittingly with a bad choice by the bridegroom. He mounted the bonnet of an old van driven by a humourless old man who did not see the funny side of things. Instead of slowing down to let him off, he accelerated up the road. The bridegroom avoided being thrown off only by leaning the weight of his torso on the roof of the van. He disappeared around the corner out of sight. There were great cheers and shouts, and some concern when he did not reappear. A few minutes later the bridegroom came running back to a hero's welcome. He was paler than he had been. But he could not miss this chance. What a culmination of the festivities: he threw his arms up as he fell into the group, cursing the old man for all he was worth. His bold gesture had almost resulted in disaster, but for that very reason it showed what a 'character' he was – how ready to take risks with his personal safety, how finely judged to just miss real calamity.

Language

More than anything else it was language and conversation which demonstrated the elaborate, ornate, indirect and stylish nature of the hippy culture. Talking was a central activity. Friends met mainly to talk and exchange recent experiences. The *crucial* thing about conversation, however, was nothing to do with the objective content of what was said. It was related to the style, movement and surprise – the *way* – in which things were said. It was the craftsmanship, grace and panache of language which was important. Content was the clay in which style was worked. Everyday life had become a kind of art.

Conversations would turn on sudden interruptions, provocative statements, sudden denials, insolent questionings, apparent paradoxes. It was the mark of the stranger or acolyte that he would try to express something directly or naïvely – especially concerning central cultural values. It was greatly appreciated when a *non sequitur*, or enigmatic statement stopped a conversation, but in an appropriate way, or transformed what had been said into something specially understood only by the head.

The real point was always the missing one or the implied one. Straights, in particular, were spoofed time and again by this. They would talk at a 'reasonable' level and desperately try to hang on to ever-receding logical threads, while the heads would grow merrier at the private meanings they were paradoxically, inconsistently and surrealistically invoking as they challenged and minced the logic of the intruder.

In these two brief exchanges caught on tape remember that Ron was essentially an outsider, a 'straight' who knew one of the heads and joined the larger group sometimes in a pad after the pub:

Ron:	I'm not saying what's right or wrong, I'm saying that there is a moral code.
Stuart:	What about a jam sandwich?
Val:	So there's a moral code.
Stuart:	What about a jam sandwich, ha ha ha ha

103

	. . . a jam sandwich on top of morals spread it out, jam and morals.
Les:	It's all to do with Manson.
Ron:	I think it's a bloody good idea [campaigns to discourage people from smoking]. . . . Of course, it is . . . and this is all anybody's trying to do, except for a small bloody silly pressure minority.
Les:	I think that carbon dioxide in three parts, nitrogen in two parts is a very good mixture of gases to breathe.
Ron:	What's that? . . .
Les:	Makes you hallucinate . . .
Stuart:	It'll also suffocate you.
Ron:	That still doesn't argue the point.

Head humour was characteristically articulated around bizarre and distorted expressions of unspoken but fundamental attitudes. This account of Les was greeted with great hilarity. It plays with, counterposes and ironically explores – never states – a number of in-group values and concerns: the weirdness of life, the unexpected, self-parody, the power of drugs, understatement, the natural turned psychedelic:

| Les: | I had a fantastic experience, I went down to Bath [Pop Festival] and I got down by the front of the audience where all the real hippies were [laughter]. We are king hippies and we got this sleeping-bag, this arctic sleeping-bag, and I was really into it, and this friend of mine went to score some shit, and he came back with the shit, and it was like really bad shit, you know, it looked like Cadbury's cocoa, and he says, he took about three drags and he said, 'It's no good.' He says, 'There's something wrong with it, it's a bum deal.' So I took about five drags and I said, 'I dunno it's quite nice' [laughter]. Then I went to sleep and I woke up in about |

fifteen minutes and I was tripping and it was
quite beautiful, man, it was mescalin in it or
something, and then Frank Zappa came on,
oh . . . it was fantastic, it blew my mind . . .
and Frank Zappa finished. Then they had
those other bands on and then it was
beautiful, sky was blue with clouds, you
know, and I was stoned, and people were
smashed and tripping and all these people
had got different colours round them, you
know. It was beautiful, then it suddenly
went dark, and I looked up, I was sort of
lying, and there was this great big cunt, oh
it was a massive cunt, man, it was beautiful
and it was just looking at me, and I was
looking back at up it, you know
[prolonged laughter]. I was really
fascinated by it, because it was sparkling
with this mescalin, fucking hell, too much,
and then it suddenly went blue sky again
[laughter]. I thought, ah, and I looked up
and there was this chick walking through the
crowd, and she stood over me for about
thirty seconds, it was mind-blowing, it
really was and she was about 30, and she
had just got this over her, it fucking blew
my head. Bath Festival was incredible, I'll
never forget that. [Laughter.]

There was a great deal of patience for a long rambling tale if it
held certain ingredients, and was expressed in culturally
appropriate manner. There was very little patience for
conventional, passed on, straight and straightforwardly told
jokes. Such tales were dimensionless, predictable and a bore.
Ron was not a head, and his outsider status was shown precisely
by his inability to tell a tale in a quirky, interesting way. His
delivery did not imply any of the richness, complexity and irony
that was at the heart of the culture. Here is Ron attempting to
tell a conventional 'funny' joke. The conditions of this
exchange were the same as those above for Les, it was late at

night and everyone was 'stoned':

Ron:	Well, there's this guy, you see, he's lying across the cinema seats, so an old woman comes along and says 'Excuse me, do you mind moving, I want to sit down'. He goes 'Argh, argh'. She says 'You've got to move, otherwise I'll call the usherette to move you'. And he goes 'Argh, argh'. So she goes off and calls the usherette. She comes along, 'Excuse me, sir, you've got to move'. And, like, he goes 'Argh'.
Les:	Hurry up, Ron.
Ron:	And, like, she goes 'Like, I'll have to call the manager'.
	The manager comes and says 'Right, sir, we can't have this', he says.
Stuart:	Oh, for fuck sake, get on with it.
Ron:	'Right, sir, we can't have this, what's your name?'. He goes 'Argh'. 'Right', he says, 'we can't have this, we're gonna call the police'. So the copper comes and he says 'Right, sir, I'm afraid I'm going to have to charge you with causing a public disturbance.'
Stuart:	Ah, come on!
Ron:	'Right, what's your name?' 'Argh.' 'OK, well, you don't have to tell me your name, where do you come from?' He goes 'Argh, argh, the balcony!'
Les:	Well, get on with this joke then.

Music and style

Music for the hippies was an immediate apprehension, itself and nothing more: it could not be presented in terms other than itself. It was impossible to decode. It could safely hold contradictory, otherwise unexpressed or profound meanings. Logocentric disbelief and derisive rationalism could be insulted. Music could never destroy spiritual suggestivity by too clear an exposure in the way that words or other symbolic and indirect mediations might have done. It communicates *directly* with the faithful:

Stuart: It's so difficult to talk about, it's not . . . [discussing an LP of Frank Zappa].

Les: It's just like trying to talk about Beefheart, you can't talk about it, you've just got to experience it.

Paul: Some of the records which demand this attention, the sound is so heavy . . . now, with this big electric guitar bit, you can't carry on talking, because it goes into your head and stops there, it's like somebody hypnotizing you, it takes you like it. You are not only listening to the record, you are in it. This is the basic difference between that and the old stuff [i.e. commercial music before the 'progressive' era of pop].

The hippies had an enormous knowledge of their field and a nuanced appreciation of the difference between various groups and styles. Their taste was in no sense bland, accidental or random. Certainly it was not commercially determined. They liked 'progressive', or 'underground' music which was not disseminated widely, and not represented in the current 'top 20s'.

The original progenitors of rock were accorded a kind of respect. Buddy Holly, early Elvis Presley, Little Richard and Chuck Berry were recognized as the authentic exponents of a tradition that was very quickly perverted by commercial pressures. The really important musical breakthrough for the hippies came with the release of *Sergeant Pepper's Lonely Heart Club Band* in 1967. This marked the break up of the old musical patterns and the old pattern of commercial management. For the first time groups had artistic self-determination. They could play what really interested them. The Beatles, for the hippies, were very soon left behind. They had merely opened people's sensibilities to what was already there (so that, for instance, Frank Zappa and the

Mothers of Invention, could now come into their own – it was claimed that Frank Zappa had been the real progenitor of underground music in his LP *Freak Out*) and what was to come. On this side of the Atlantic, there was the blues-influenced, 'heavy', guitar-based line of Cream, Hendrix and Led Zeppelin; and on the other side of the Atlantic, there was the 'West-coast sound', 'acid rock', more overtly based on acid and psychedelia, but still using very powerful rock rhythms. For the hippies the big names in the West-coast sound were the Grateful Dead, Jefferson Airplane, the Doors and Country Joe and the Fish. Frank Zappa was seen as presiding over the whole underground scene in a way that defied classification. The English group Pink Floyd were seen as the distinctive exponents of an English tradition of acid music, a much more way-out and cerebralized version of American acid rock.

Subsequent worthwhile music was seen as a development from, or combination of, these main lines. Flock, Led Zeppelin, Blind Faith, Canned Heat, Van Morrison, Emerson, Lake and Palmer were all liked to varying degrees, but rarely so much as the 'masters': Hendrix, Zappa, Country Joe MacDonald, Grace Slick, John Mayall.

Being a 'head'

The notion of being a 'head' catches very well the central features of the hippy style. Interaction, and communication generally, was unpredictable and quirky: reminiscent at the extremes of the psychotic – the *head* case. But this inconsistency was only registered as arbitrariness on the *outside*. The 'real head' was appreciated precisely because he operated within the *genre* of 'the mad' – he was a 'freak' – but in a *style* which *at the same time* mocked conventional values and implied a superior vision. Their behaviour was in this sense double coded, so that what was incoherent behaviour to one set of observers – straight society – could also be deeply meant and meaningful behaviour to another set of observers – the 'heads'. But the knowingness of the 'head' could never be directly expressed for that would have dispelled the aura of the mad. Contradiction, denial, the unpredictable, the unexpected, ironic detachment, could all operate intricately and suggestively within their own culture, but they could *also* be taken as 'mad', 'freakish' and quite random by the 'straight'. So in a crucial sense the head was a 'head case', and conventional society was accurate in its assessment, *within its own perspective*. But this 'madness' was welcomed and intricately exploited at the level of style by the hippies to express – in a way no other medium could so richly allow – something both of their disdain for conventional society and its public definitions, and of their *private* reach for the inexpressible.

That the notion of the 'head' was at the centre of the hippy consciousness, and the seat of many of their feelings is shown by the range of uses the word had in their vocabulary. 'Head' was used to express just about every aspect of their sensibilities. It was used to denote political beliefs, 'Where most straights' heads are', and taste in music, 'My head's really into that'. It was used in a macro-sense to demonstrate wholesale symbolic affinity, 'There's some real heads in suits with short hair', and even as a metaphor for the spirituality of all mankind, 'Humanity's head's in a very nice state'. It was used to denote stages of personal development, 'Where my head is now', and to suggest empathic states, 'I know what his head's into'. 'Head' was also used to express every state of emotion and especially to express extreme emotion, 'It freaks you right out of your head'. Finally, it was used to describe just about every form of drug use, and it was in this area that widespread use of the word first developed, 'He's a lush-head, an acid-head, a pill-head, an H-head', etc. It was almost as if the hippy really *was* just his head, and feelings and experiences just forms of abstract awareness located in the *head*. Les said often: 'It's all head games on the scene, man, that's all you need to understand.'

Distinction from the 'straights' and dead-centre cultural feelings were, therefore, based most importantly on this sense of being 'a head'. It was understanding that category which placed you on the inside. For instance, a barman at the Anchor aspired to join the hippies but was never accepted because he was not a 'head'. He was *too* serious, *too* full of innocent mimicry, *too* straightforward, *too* healthy, *too* much in the real world, *too* literal in his interpretations, *too* enthusiastic, *too* ready to laugh without irony. He had not realized that the essential requirement for membership was not belief, *readiness* or willingness, but *style* – a *patterning* of existence, the mannered greeting of a complex fate. When Stuart flicked beer at the barman, the barman flicked it right back good-naturedly. When Stuart refused to drink up before all the tables were wiped and cleaned, the barman *wiped* the tables and came back again to further prevarications. He followed all kinds of literal instructions and conditions while the metaphoric secret of being a 'head' eluded him. All his approaches were marked with a similar over-reaction to surface reality, to the tracings over assumed meanings.

On the other hand, 'straights' could behave in a head fashion even though they had no apparent cultural affinities with, or aspirations towards, the hippies. One day before the hippy wedding, there was a large group sitting in the Anchor discussing the wedding. Somebody knew a 'straight' standing at the bar and he was half-jokingly trying to persuade the 'straight' to come to see what a hippy wedding was like. The 'straight' looked uncertain and said there was 'something else' he had to do that Saturday, but that he would certainly try to come. The whole group had overheard this exchange during a lull in the conversation, and one of the heads said slowly and emphatically, expecting to be appreciated, 'Nothing has precedence over anything else except for a good crap'. There was much laughter: a point had been made. In the 'straight' world 'affairs' might prevent you from doing what you wanted, but in the 'hip' world you could please yourself. Only natural imperatives, not artificial, social ones constructed the day. The 'straight' looked taken aback, and paused while the laughter continued, but then he did something which was sufficiently unexpected, and unlikely, though oddly relevant, to completely turn the tables – 'I can be a head, too'. He slowly and meticulously took his wallet from his inside pocket, opened it with exaggerated care, and took out a perfectly folded piece of paper that for all the world could have been a business letter. It was not, it was toilet paper, and he showed it around and gave it to the speaker without saying a word. It was later agreed that this was 'one of the best put-downs ever', and the incident was often described afterwards.

The sense of community

There was a sense of community among the hippies but it would be misrepresented by the vocabulary of 'love', 'peace' and 'brotherhood'. The sense of community was based more on shared understandings of a *precarious* life-project rather than on a conscious espousal of a confidently felt alternative.

The basic element of fellowship was commented upon by the local vicar:

> There's this kind of thing, you see, where they're trying to work out by themselves something informal, but it's quite surprising how happy they are when they're in a group. Very much a social thing. Again this is another aspect of it, they are the sort of people who are living a group-centred existence for their own security, whereas most people around here, for example, this road, er, people will sort of pop out of their doors but will pop in again more quickly than they popped out.

And even the drug squad grudgingly admitted something of the same:

> A: They accept anyone . . . the people who have got the hippy philosophy, as you call it . . . their philosophy is to be friendly with anyone, and if somebody wants a bed or a cup of tea or something like that they will accept them into their pads, and by doing so they are getting people in there who are rooking them left right and centre, conning them, never mind them conning the villains.

It was frequently commented: 'People really look after you in the village.' If you had no money you could always get something to eat, a drink or a smoke or a room for the night. Outsiders often paid a kind of toll-gate fee in acts of generosity in the Anchor. For instance, two merchant seamen turned up while I was working on the scene. They were always buying drinks, and gave several packets of cigarettes away. The hippies freely accepted this generosity without any of the conventional embarrassment, or ritual disclaimers, expected in 'straight' society.

In a more general sense there was a widespread sense of belonging to an easily identifiable social group. Many of the hippies were 'on the road'. They always felt certain of a welcome 'amongst our own kind'. This was an exclusive thing. If you did not look right, you would not be accepted:

Stuart: You get a guy that looks like any of us, barring Ron . . . you can go into any decent-sized town, and find your kind of people, now Ron would have a lot more trouble.

Ron: Because I don't wear the uniform.

Stuart: Because basically he dresses smart, he wears suits, shirts, ties, he'd find it a lot more difficult.

Ron: I haven't got the uniform.

Stuart: He hasn't got the uniform, so there's still this. . . .

Les: This is an interesting facet, isn't it? The skinheads and the greasers can't go from territory to territory and be accepted. We can go anywhere and get accepted, you know by our own folk.

Stuart: Yes, very true.

It was felt that a hippy could be certain of a welcome, even across national and language barriers. The hippy movement was felt to be truly international:

Robin: On the continent again, I'm still pretty full of it, I wander through a strange town, and everybody is hostile except the people with long hair . . . and the people with long hair are people like me, in to my thing or almost or somewhere related . . . you're wandering into a town, and it's nightfall and you have got nowhere to stay that night and you want somewhere to crash, you can't go up to short-haired people and ask . . . you seek out the long hair . . . but if I had short hair,

they are not going to trust me, they are not
going to be willing to make that contact.

However, this sense of community was not as wholesome as
the 'straight' world sometimes imagines. 'Love' and 'peace'
would only have a totally positive meaning in the 'straight'
world which takes these 'values' – though unattainable – as
real, obvious and self-explanatory. The local vicar, from his own
perspective, hinted at something of the ambiguous nature of
the hippy community spirit:

> At the drop of a hat they will do their most caring work, and
> do a damn sight more than most people would, but I haven't
> seen enough of this to work out in my own mind the reason
> behind it. Is it because they really care, or is it because of the
> pressures and the general insecurity, they fling themselves
> into one another . . . they are not caring for each other
> because they are stable and emotionally whole, but they're
> caring in order to bolster one another up.

In a tangential way this corroborates my analysis. In a real
sense the hippies were insecure, but instead of this being an
unavoidable evil as the vicar suggests, it was *welcomed* and
experimented with. The sense of community was the sense of
others being engaged in a similar experiment, enjoying similar
insights, sharing common, though often unexpressed, views on
the nature of existence. Only with people who shared the same
symbolic atmosphere could there be meaningful interaction.
Only with the *sharing* of assumptions could those assumptions
be exquisitely shaped and presented as style. Only with those
who accepted the shadowy world, the darker side of experience,
could conventionally 'weird' behaviour develop and flower into
ironic, complex statements about life. If 'straights' came too far
into the scene, it froze the movement and grace of the culture.
It threatened to import unavoidable definitions from the
outside world; with too many carriers of the real world around
there might be real madness instead of merely a mad style. So
instead of the sense of community being the romantic one of
full-blooded love and peace bringing a new age, it was more one
of a decisive rejection of 'straights' and the erection of a barrier
against their polluting definitions. The hippies' sense of

community came from a collective conspiracy to hold their world as 'real', rather than from the pure altruism of 'love' and 'peace'.

Thus, despite the sense of community, there was a disconcerting indifference about individuals and their welfare. If somebody were in trouble they would be helped, and 'hip' people were always preferable to 'straights', but there was no concern for, or even interest in, particular life-trajectories. Individuals would disappear from the scene overnight without a word, or ripple of concern. You could have someone staying in your pad for months and they could leave at a moment's notice without regrets. It was possible to be in a sexual relationship and call it off in a moment without feeling, or expecting recrimination. Calamities and terrible misfortunes befalling others were witnessed without great emotion. Concern was always tinged with 'It's their thing, leave them free to experience it.'

This sense of community as a structured *dépasse* of conventional reality, rather than as a positive enactment of brotherhood, allows us to understand why there were far fewer genuine communes than there were houses simply shared. Individuals came to be living together often through *lack of feasible alternative*. It was hard to get back into a conventional society, to recross into a reality which might define you as mad.

4   Control agencies as cultural participants and locators of significance

An interesting aspect of the hippy culture was that one of its central cultural items around which complex and developed meanings were dialectically spun – drugs – was the object of massive police control measures. We have here an archetypal example of the relation between the controlled and the controllers, and more particularly of the cultural consequences of this for the meanings surrounding the items in dispute between them.[3] There are sub-plots and hidden patterns beneath the more obvious power relations in our society which are actually more responsible than the public and visible transactions for the production of lived meanings and some forms of social long-term stability.

The city drug squad maintained a permanent contact with the hippy scene, but they had little understanding of the hippy philosophy, or at best a partial, cynical perspective across it. They thought that the hippies used their dress and style to cover up laziness and inadequacy and that many hippies were disturbed mentally. An accurate perception of the psychotic element in the hippy style, but without an appreciation of its context and meaning, led to a *pathological* view of the whole culture. The drug squad were relieved from the effort to find an internal validity in the culture precisely because they could understand it all as a product of illness. Drugs, in particular, were used, they believed, to compensate for mental instability.

The drug squad's perspective was, of course, necessarily and understandably limited by its material and organizational location. They measured 'success' in terms of people *leaving* the scene and coming off drugs. Their job was to limit drug-use generally. Their account to themselves of the culture could hardly be favourable in view of these objectives:[4]

A: The trouble is this, we only signify their measure of success by when they come off the scene, and move out into normal social-type activities, that's what we consider an achievement, maybe we don't know what they've achieved.

B: I feel, quite honestly, that they use it [the philosophy] as an excuse for their way of life, because logically, if you look at it logically, it isn't a logical reason for their way of life at all. You can still be just as strong living against or for something living what we believe to be a normal life. I don't say that they don't think their way of life is normal.

A: They want to live without working, or they want a form of association with people who are living without working, when it's a form of escapism so far as some people are concerned, and then on the other hand, you

115

can pull more birds if you're hippy, if you're in their particular state of mind and their particular state of dress, their talk will encourage young girls to come. If they were dressed in normal dress, then they would be inadequate personalities and nobody would take any notice of them, but because of the mere fact that they are 'way out', people take an interest in them, and this is where the contacts are made.

These views are clear and demonstrate a fundamentally critical attitude. When we come, however, to the drug squad's *actual* approach to, and interaction with, the hippies, there was not a consistent working out of these attitudes. The drug squad were distinctly friendly to the hippies, and expected, and often received, a friendliness from them in return. There was pride taken in the fact that if 'you went up to them and said "I'm a bit down this week"', they'd give you a couple of quid just like that'. Even more surprisingly the drug squad felt that this friendship could hold even after a 'bust' – 'If you put a chap away and he knows he's in the wrong, I hope he can go down for a year, eighteen months, whatever it is, and come out and say hello to me afterwards, it's having a relationship isn't it?' The people I spoke to in the drug squad knew hundreds of individuals personally around the scene, including *all* of the individuals I worked with. The interaction with these individuals was, in the drug squad's own words, 99 per cent unrelated to drugs, and the drug squad, though it was not said in so many words, clearly turned a blind eye to many small offences. It was perfectly obvious to the drug squad that people they talked to in the clubs and the pubs usually had dope on them, but what was the use of 'knocking some young kid off, you couldn't go there again'? Reading between the lines, it is clear that 'busts' were carefully regulated rather than the *automatic* consequences of detection and tip-offs. To have come down too heavily, and too consistently would have forced relationships beyond breaking-point. A diplomatic eye of restraint was kept on 'busts' that would seriously affect 'friendly relations'.

Members of the drug squad spent hours around the hippy
haunts, and made no attempt to conceal their identity. On the
contrary, they sometimes used their institutional position as a
joke to further the friendliness of interaction. One of the drug
squad officers told me that he had gone into the Anchor, stood
in the centre of the bar with his hands behind his back, and
with a slight bending of the knees, intoned 'Good evening, all',
in an explicit take-off of the most famous of all English police
stereotypes. This same incident was recounted to me by the
hippies. They thought the officer was 'quite a character': they
felt predisposed to trust and welcome him.

The friendliness of the drug squad was *generally* reciprocated.
The hippies said that they quite liked individuals on the squad,
understood that they were 'just doing a job', and sympathized
with some of their actions:

Stuart:	I often talk with them, I find them very nice people . . . they're just doing a job. . . .
Les:	If you're cheeky with them they don't like it, I mean to say, would you, somebody taking the piss out of you all the time, and it was in your power to do something about it, wouldn't you do something? It's human nature . . . but if you like a guy, you leave him alone.

It was widely believed in the culture that if you kept yourself to
yourself, you would not be busted:

Stuart:	. . . they know you smoke, they know you don't just tat about with it, as long as you keep yourself to yourself, keep your mouth shut.
Les:	Don't make a big scene about it.
Stuart:	Don't go screaming and shouting it from the roof-tops, do it quietly in your own flat, or at a friend's pad, then they'll leave you alone . . . you start smoking in the street or the pub and they will bust you, it's obvious what they're going to do.
Les:	That's the drug squad in relation to us, I

> think you know that in relation to the
> horsehead they give them a fucking bad
> time, I feel sorry for a horsehead, and
> spades, they give them a rough time,
> unfairly so . . . they just put it down to
> doing their job, if we play their little game,
> they leave us alone.

Occasionally the drug squad were seen as positively helpful.
Les explained how there had been a guy with 'a shooter' around
on the scene, 'pushing stuff and demanding money, crazy, he
could have murdered somebody'. There was nobody who could
handle such a situation, so Les and a few others spoke to the
drug squad and 'the guy was lifted'. There was also an
occasional problem on the scene when a supplier or pusher 'got
too heavy'. This could take many forms, perhaps the most
common was where a pusher supplied unlimited drugs to an
individual, often a girl, got her into debt, and demanded
repayment which could often only be met by the girl herself
pushing drugs to third parties. In this way an enterprising
pusher could build up a small empire and push himself more
towards the supply end of the drugs trade which, of course,
carried much more substantial profits. Simple physical coercion
was sometimes used, or individuals might be drawn into a
network through the power of a dominating personality, or a
sexual liaison. Whatever the exact form, the only real way for
the individual to escape these pressures was to alert the drug
squad in some way. This could take the form of 'setting up' the
pusher – giving police exact information about where the
pusher could be 'busted' with the maximum possible
incriminating evidence. More commonly the individual would
make a show of getting in touch with the squad – be seen
talking to them – so that the pusher would 'get the message'
that further pressure might bring the drug squad down on
him.

There was sometimes a real sense of gratitude to the drug
squad among groups and individuals where someone had been
'saved' from domination by hard drugs. Everybody on the scene
recognized that 'H' could be a dangerous thing. The hippy
attitude was that if people wanted to use it, and they knew the

risks, then they should be allowed 'to get on with it', but they also respected the drug squad's view of the situation, and believed that they had prevented some people from dying. It was also widely thought that the drug squad was 'only really interested' in smashing the big H-pushers: this was seen as a partly legitimate task.

It must be recognized that in a crucial sense both the drug squad and the hippies shared a culture – though they understood it differently. They were in a position over both against prison and the formal structure of the law. Despite the drug squad's critical view of the hippy philosophy, they were, nevertheless, part of the wider culture and supported some of its central social meanings.

Of course, this cultural membership posed a number of problems and contradictions for the police; as one of them said: 'It's not logical, but it's got a kind of logic . . . it's not the case, just a case of following the laws and locking people up . . . it's not strictly logical but it has its own sense.'

The basic contradiction the drug squad had to live through was in satisfying the demands of law-enforcement while preserving a minimum cultural membership. If the police had applied the full strength of the law on every occasion, they would soon have been rejected by the hippies. On the other hand, they could not long justify their role as police if they made no arrests.

Another contradiction facing the individual drug squad policeman was one of personal morality – he was both friend and traitor to his contacts in the culture. There *was* a sense of friendship on both sides, but in the last analysis the friendship was only entered into, from the police side, in order to get information which could well *damage* the contact. One of the drug squad said to me, in the same breath as evoking his friendship for the hippies, 'but if anyone trusts me he's a fool'.

What was the purpose of all this? Why did the drug squad put themselves in this tight circle between the demands of law enforcement and the requirements of a cultural membership? Why did they put themselves in a position of moral duplicity? We can understand their behaviour by appreciating that they were not aiming to eradicate drug use and to solve the problem once and for all. They did not see the hippies as implacable enemies who had to be eliminated at all costs. The drug squad's real function was to control and regulate the culture, to keep it within safe bounds and to make sure that it did not radically affect, influence or inconvenience other areas of society:[5]

A: It's dealing with the whole problem. I'll tell you how we measure our success, it's not busts, it's the number of people admitted to the Royal after a weekend, that's a real measure of what we do. . . . We're keeping a regular pressure on the culture, controlling, containing it, building a wall around it, we can't stop the people who are involved, but can prevent others getting in.

A direct assault on the culture, an attempt to *eradicate* drug-taking, would in some ways have been a more straightforward job for the drug squad. They would have simply needed a lot of tough men, and wide powers of entry and arrest. The attempt to *control* and *govern* the sub-culture meant that it had to be infiltrated. The basic elements of the situation had to be understood, individuals had to be known – it was important to know 'who was conning you, and who you could trust'. All this required that the police should move in the culture, be accepted, and learn to feel the pulse of the whole scene.

Of course, there were still strong-arm jobs to be done. The large importer, or dangerous ambitions in a pusher threatening to destroy the balance of the scene would attract decisive 'unfriendly' action. It was noticeable that there was a range of personnel in the squad, from the 'hard men' who despised all drug-takers and wanted to enforce the law to the last degree to the 'softies' who were very uncertain that the law had a place in the treatment of the 'problem'. The first group could not 'fraternize' with the hippies – they did not have the social skills nor the motivation. They wanted to proceed in terms of large set actions, with several police blocking the exits of a place while suspects were searched. The second group prided themselves on their ability to 'get on with people' and preferred to work alone in a culture, 'busting' people only as a last resort. It was clear that the head of the drug squad applied the two wings of his organization differentially so that the 'hard' men were sent on 'strong-arm' jobs, and the 'soft' men were sent out for information and infiltration duties.

These were the *police* motives for seeking a minimum cultural membership, why did the hippies allow them an entry? Why voluntarily agree to a relationship based on the desire to harm you? Why accept the moral duplicity of a friendliness that could send you to jail? The ready acceptance by the hippies of the drug squad puzzled me greatly during the early stages of the research, partly because my own involvement also made me a target for the police: the *last* people I wanted to notice me. My fear of the drug squad and consternation at the way the hippies welcomed them into their culture shows the distance between my social perspective and that of the hippies. The contrast and relationship helped to point up the realization that their willingness to interact with the drug squad was *another* way of reinforcing their cultural identity, and of reaffirming certain of their attitudes, assumptions and significances. Drug use helped to symbolically separate the hippies from the 'straights'. Part of this *subjective* sense of separation was the feeling of danger involved in taking drugs. This danger was partly in what the drugs might do to you, but it was also in the social danger: you might be caught, stigmatized, even ostracized. But the hippy was already these things: these were the external dimensions of his symbolic passage. So the hippy could face down these dangers, enjoy them in a bold resonation of his cultural identity, shame the 'straight' world by courting the devil – 'supping with a very *short* spoon'. The drug squad were aware of this whole dimension and sometimes played on it to their own advantage:

A: There's an excitement in taking drugs, and they talk to us, 'cause it makes it more exciting, you know the worst you can do is to deflate them, is to take away the importance, say to a junkie, 'Go on, get a fix, you can die for all I care.'

There was also a sense in which the *power* of drugs was magnified by the drug squad's activities. That society felt it necessary to take action against drugs indicated to the hippies that drugs were powerful agents of some kind. The hippies were cashing this social significance by directly associating with the carriers and coiners of these meanings about drugs. It was especially mind-blowing to talk to a member of the drug squad when you were 'high' – you could not place yourself more beyond the 'straights'.

The drug squad were then part of the cultural configuration: high priests of some of its importances. They were not alien oppressors. For the hippies when people were 'sent down', it was not so much that the squad had acted cruelly and unilaterally so much that the whole culture – hippies and police – had decided upon a sacrificial lamb to offer 'straight' society: to keep society from mounting a real effort to destroy the culture. If you were busted, you just accepted it, you 'didn't rock the boat'. It was the *occasional* price to pay for a *general* freedom to smoke and live within the significances of the culture – significances partly maintained by the presence and actions of the drug squad.

Given this symbiotic relation of meaning and intention concerning the central role of drugs in the culture, the hippies were relatively content to accept the drug squad as controllers in a more general sense. The drug squad regulated the scene, they kept a reassuring *balance*, they were the – at any rate, nearly – impartial powerful who could enact a vendetta or protect from a beating. Agents of control can, in this way, *carry* and maintain internal cultural meanings. The drug squad were allowed a cultural role, they were used to further differentiate the culture from others in an *internally relevant* way. That the controllers may have a critical account of what motivates the 'deviants' is not really germane, if they do have a mode of cultural contact, if they can play out a relevant internal cultural role for the 'deviant' group. It is not surprising that agents of social control should legitimate their institutionally controlled objectives by criticism of the 'deviant' but this theoretical knowledge need not prevent a complex *modus vivendi* developing between the control agency and the deviant group which does not imply automatic deterioration and hostility of relations.[6] Where such a vicious circle is most likely to develop is where the controllers not only have a critical theory concerning the deviants, but no cultural contact or sympathy, and where they are unwilling to play a consistent humanized role which might allow an induction of their presence into the inner stable workings of the culture. This induction may not quite be within the terms of the agent's self-understanding, but this is not crucial so long as a stable interaction is allowed.

Where the drug squad were acceptable, the 'straight' police were despised by the hippies. They were not part of the culture, did not attempt to make friendly contacts, and did not have any kind of understanding of the privileged role of drugs in the culture. For the normal police the hippies were opaque, objectionable 'unwashed bums'. The hippies hated the police for this imputed lack of respect before their culture. The straight police did not carry importances and significances in a carefully regulated way, they simply destroyed:

Les:	Now the 'straight' fuzz, you know, they're just bastards, and they'll pick locks off your front door, they'll come creeping round the house in the middle of the night because it's happened here, you know, they'll threaten you, they'll do you over, give you a hiding because they're used to dealing with . . .
Stuart:	You come out the pub late, you've had a few bevvies, and unless you can walk down that road and keep your gob shut, they'll kick hell out of you, and that happened New Year to one guy, came out, had a few bevvies, New Year's Eve, they picked him up, because you know he'd had a few too many, dragged him off . . . and the drug squad wouldn't do that.
Les:	They're [the drug squad] moving within a sub-culture and they know it, and they know to behave like a pig doesn't get the best results.

Antagonisms and dislikes could mount with an incredible swiftness with uniformed police. We could venture a guess that if the normal police had been the main agents of control on the scene there would have been a much more paranoic polarization and hardening of attitudes.

The role of the church was somewhat similar to that of the drug squad on the scene, although of vastly smaller importance. The local vicar had objectives which were very similar to those of the drug squad: 'You see success in – in that part of – with whatever group you are dealing with, are those who eventually reach a level of stability, and move out, that's success.' This long-term aim inhibited a real understanding: most people on the scene were seen as compensating for some inadequacy. However, despite this, the church acted, in effect, to increase the hippy sense of self-importance. To start with, the mere interest of the church implied that they were a special group. Second, the church had a way of presenting and defending a simplified schematic, popular version of the hippy philosophy, which gave publicity to, and encouraged the identity and distinctiveness of, the culture. Here is an extract from a letter written by the local vicar to the *Church Times* (12 September 1969):

> I work among hippies in our Parish, and can say that many of their protests (though not all) are justified. Many protests are individual, the cry against parents who are concerned but with their own status, and who love but only with strings attached, the place of Further Education that is concerned with its system and not the people it is teaching, the Clergyman who has such rigid ideas that they cannot contain his son, the parents who were not responsible enough to say no at an early stage.

This simplification of the philosophy was partly due to a desire to find Christian principles at work in all things. It sometimes led to heightened expectations which laid the ground for many disappointments. But if Christian love partly blinded cultural understanding, it gave enormous strength to face the costs of such misunderstanding. The simplifications and optimistic approaches of the church were, therefore, peculiarly dogged, and implied something of permanence and significance within the culture beyond its actual resources so as, in the end, to become paradoxically itself one of its supports.

5   Radical life-styles and radical politics

The hippies clearly held up a bold and alternative mode of
living. It was predicated on a critique of conventional society.
Unfortunately that critique remained silent, and finally,
tragically, unorganized. There was no political analysis or
expression behind the radical life-style.

Certainly their morality was unconventional. Notions of right
or wrong, failure or success, were completely relativized.
Individual appropriateness was the main legitimation of their
ethical system:

Stuart: There's only, what you do to you is you, and
              has got nothing to do with anyone else,
              you wanna slash your wrists, you can pump
              H up your arm, although I don't agree
              with it, you wanna do it, and you're a
              responsible adult, you can do it for all I care.

Val: You've got your morals, everybody's got
              morals, the point is that nobody's morals are
              exactly the same, so it's just a drag trying to
              decide whether one's right or wrong.

There was a profound opposition to the materialism of
modern society – especially in relation to their own spiritual
feelings:

Les: It's a paranoic system, they're conditioned
              to think they've got to get something better
              all the time, but what they think is better is
              material things. The conditioned think that
              material things are better looking, there's
              this whole sort of, I don't want to sound coy,
              but the spiritual concepts you know, I think
              everyone needs, this is my personal opinion,
              and not everyone needs this is obvious by
              society, but for me I need the spiritual side
              of life. I'm not saying that I believe in God
              or anything like that, but I do need the
              spiritual side and I think this is what society

125

expressly does not provide for at the
moment.

Their whole culture was often seen by the hippies as a
subversive force working away at the roots of conventional
society. The culture was most successful in weakening
conventional society by taking its children, both because this
took away future leaders and workers, but also, and most
enjoyably, because it enraged the parents and older generation.
The archetypal case of this mischievous attack from within was
the seduction of the 'straight' young girl, an amazingly popular
and continually reworked image among the hippies. For the
heads, 'straight' society was paranoic mainly because of its
attempt to control and hide its own nature, frustrations, desires
from itself. This repression was symbolized most profoundly in
society's attempt to protect the purity of its daughters. By taking
this purity the hippies penetrated the inner sanctum of the
straight world. At one stroke the whole symbolic complex of
deferred gratification, restraint and control, standards, earned
pleasure, respect, manners could be brought down:

Les: It's beautiful, man [the *OZ* trial], it's the
best thing that could happen, it's brilliant,
the media's gonna get hold of this, man.
You know what they are going to do with it,
don't you? – there's gonna be one hell of a
shout, man, this purveyor of pornography,
corrupting their 13-year-old daughters. And
then it gets in the fucking press man, you
know, and you get pictures of fucking
'hippies', and then all the people walking
down the road think 'The bastards are
screwing our 13-year-old daughters now'.
It's too fucking much . . . it really is.

Individually, then, and through their culture, the hippies
acted out a genuine alternative. In many important ways their
life-style implied a decisive rejection of capitalism as such. Some
commentators have argued that the hippy style in general was in
a dialectical relationship with the revolutionary left, an
alternative manifestation of a similar political mood.[7]

While not doubting the strength and authenticity of the hippy style; and while not doubting the huge influence it has had on young people; and while not underestimating the importance of a radical experimentation with whole life-style, rather than with mere political rhetoric, we cannot proclaim the identity of the hippy interest with that of the political left. In many important ways the culture was tragically limited precisely by an inability to push through to the politically radical – the only grounds on which it could create conditions for its own long-term survival. As it was many of the important elements of the culture remained incompatible with a progressive political perspective. The distinctive contradiction of the hippy movement is its combination of an undoubtedly radical style with political attitudes which are finally far from radical.

Their idealist notion of organic individualism set them against collectivized perspectives. The failings of modern society were measured against *this* model. Capitalism was opposed in so far as it removed the individual sensibility from its natural and proper home – the organically relevant and densely celled, *natural* community:

Robin: I'd like to go back say 2000 years and start all over again, on the sort of pastoral level, avoid the industrial things, avoiding large mistakes, I see this as the ideal and it's not possible with things as they are. Now, you know, people aren't aware, in its broadest sense, they're not aware, they're blind, deaf, dumb and insensitive. . . . You know, reduce the world's population by 300,000,000, and drop a trip of acid on everyone that's left . . . you know, I believe that, I'm sure it's right, if you make people aware of things and there are few enough of them, then you can get together, and do something constructive rather than destructive, which is what's been happening for the last 4000 years.

The hippies were not, in any obvious sense, committed to redistribution of wealth. Europe was already 'worked out' for

them. This was at least partly due to the way democratic reforms
had smoothed out the contours of underprivilege. In a way the
material aspects of poverty were a contingency for the hippies.
The central thing was the quality and richness of experience and
this was often enacted *precisely* through spiritual aspects of
poverty. The move from the scruffy terrace/local street, and all
the human density that implied, to the new tower
block/impersonal highway, and the human desolation that
implied, was paralleled for the hippies in the gigantic move of
the whole of Europe from an older hierarchic, ornate order to a
standardized, affluent, democratic drabness. In the dust and
poverty of India the hippy hoped to find those spiritual values
and authentic experiences that were so spectacularly lacking in
the West. There was a feeling that poverty was inextricably
bound up with these treasures.

The attitude to women in the culture was far from
progressive. They had a place which was certainly different
from, and usually inferior to, men. They could be most
fulfilled, it was thought, by living out what was taken as their
'natural' and 'intrinsic' selves. Generally, the hippies distrusted
the women's movement, and contrasted its ideals with their
notion of the *natural* female and her organic role:

Les:	They[young girls] become women and everything a woman means, 'cause it means a lot to me, I don't know about you, you know, women nowadays are trying to compete with men at their level, but, you know, I don't think many head chicks do this. I think, you know, they're just in for the women at their level, sort of being complementary to each other and I don't think the materialistic society quite fully appreciates it. I can see evidence that it doesn't.
PW:	I'm not quite with you.
Les:	You know women try to be sort of career women.
PW:	Well, how about equality?
Les:	Crap, isn't it, you know.

Stuart:	There's no such thing.
Val:	If they were meant to be men, they'd be born men.
Les:	Why be equal? Why not become complementary, I think it's just that these chicks are being screwed by some bastard in their earlier life, because they've got a very warped view of life in my opinion. You know, this is just my opinion, I mean if somebody had sort of gone to this chick when he first screwed her and screwed her with absolûte tenderness, and showed the quality of fucking love as much as he could, they wouldn't have been freaking out all over the place, wanting equal fucking rights, you know. They just want to be into being women, because it's a beautiful fucking thing.

Their use of drugs also decisively separated them from activist left-wing groups and limited the hippies' political potential. Drugs put them through a symbolic barrier into a subjective world which underwrote their sense of the unreality of things, and of their powerlessness to affect the 'real' world. Drug-taking also induced a release from personal guilt and a general sense of being determined which made political action irrelevant and anyway impossible. It is no accident that certain radical groups outlaw drug-taking. It unhinges the power of action and blunts the sharpness of anger.

The hippies' general emphasis on the importance of subjective experience capsized any *theoretical* knowledge they possessed of inequality and exploitation. It did not matter if one were exploited so long as the *experience* of the situation was pleasant. They operated at a 'different' level from 'normal' people and they could never really be exploited within their own terms. This was nowhere more apparent than in their attitude to work – the crucial site of any revolutionary analysis or action:

Les:	I think that anybody that does work justifies that work. Not only does he justify it as though it's something to be done, but he

gets a certain amount of pleasure. You take
any work situation, like a mechanic at a
garage, right. Now, he's got his little perks,
he's flogging his fucking sparking-plugs on
the side for about five bob for four or
something like that, and he's nicking a bit
of oil, right, he's flogging that out, and he's
doing up his own car, right, after hours,
little fiddles like this. He's got a place where
he sits down and he skives for most of the
day, it's a big garage, now he's made that
fucking work situation into a kind of social
existence, he's justified it, and he's got the
best end of the fucking both worlds for him
in that situation. Now, you can take a
fucking nightwatchman, and they get shit
man, they are paid fucking shit, you'd
probably get more off the fucking labour
than a nightwatchman does, so OK, he goes
down there, he starts at 7 o'clock, so he goes
down the boozer and he has a couple of
fucking pints, and he comes up at about 9
o'clock. Then he lights his fucking lamps on
the road, and then he goes back down the
boozer for a night-cap and he comes up and
he stokes up his fire, and he does his fucking
toast and cheese, and it's fucking great,
have you ever tasted toast and cheese done
on a brazier? It's beautiful, man, that cat's
really living. So OK, he says good-night to
everybody, walking home from the pub, you
know, and he has his little chats, and he gets
quiet about 12 o'clock, so he rolls his coat
up, eyes down-looking puts his sun-glasses
on, wakes up about 5 o'clock the next
morning with the birds, stokes up his
fucking fire again, 'cos he's freezing cold,
does himself some breakfast, and he clocks
off the job at 8 o'clock . . . the guy's living
and he's enjoying it, and everybody's

fucking enjoying it, and you get the bigger
the corporation, the bigger the fucking
enjoyment, have you ever noticed that? You
take the Army, the Navy or the Air Force,
they are really into some fucking scenes,
those cats, their meaningful work probably
takes five minutes a day, or a week, in the
Army their meaningful work. . . . What
I'm saying essentially is that work is a
monstrous, ludicrous, fucking game, and it
takes a fucking head to realize it. . . . You
know, I fucking realize it. I'm going to
treat work as a fucking game, but I don't
give a fuck what anyone says if I get a job.
I'm going to enjoy the game, or I don't
work, you know. It's just something, it's
like you got a Monopoly set, and you can
play or you needn't play, you've got a
decision to make.

Such a non-labour-based notion of 'value' and such a
contingent view of exploitation is disorganized from within any
kind of revolutionary analysis, even though, paradoxically,
it can be understood as an experimentation with *post*-
revolutionary themes, feelings and attitudes. There was
nothing in the hippy repertoire, however, to bring about this
revolution, and nothing in the left-wing repertoire to connect
with their experimental and experiential enactments of
post-revolutionary scenarios.

The points at which the radical left critique is likely to
impinge on capitalism *coincide* with those of the hippy
critique – they have the same objects, but this does not mean
that the analyses from which they sprang are the same, or that
final objectives are the same.

Of course, one difficulty is in delineating just what is the
organized revolutionary left's notion of the new society. The
alternative hippy life-style constitutes a mute though
devastating condemnation of the cultural bankruptcy of the far
left. The new society need not necessarily be the drab,
standardized or minimizing thing which the hippies frequently

caricatured it as. Evidently, the left-wing commitment is that the final communist society would liberate man's true *human* potential in massive diversity. However, for the hippy, such a society – in the absence of any countervailing statements – did seem to be based on rationalism, scientificism, equality, clarity, and on the *suppression* of superstition, hierarchy, mannerism, élitism and all the visible frills of privilege. The revolutionary move was seen as a narrowing of the range of human experience – no matter if the lost margins contained also human injustice. The move was seen as away from idiosyncrasy, anomaly and mystery. Now it was in all these shadowy areas, which scientific materialism would have took them from, that the hippy felt most at home. It was in these settings that the game could best be played out, and the search for elusive transcendence continued. Irrationality, suspended logic, superstition were vital, for, without these things, a *resolution* would be forced, an end-game played out, which would once and for all reduce spiritual aspiration. For the hippy, the new society would not have allowed the shadows, the nooks and crannies, in which to play unnecessary games. The clear sunlight would have cruelly picked out the mad in a style which, in the shadows, was rich, dense and confident.

This may risk overinterpretation, but certainly the hippy dislike and distrust of the 'political type', and of their version of communism, was striking. This was typical:

Tony: There's no room for me in communism . . .
          no room for me as an individual, you know,
          if I wanted to do something, you know, I'd
          have less freedom in a communist society.
          . . . I could never get on with it, you know,
          I couldn't work for the society, I could only
          ever work for me, you know. . . . There's
          no room for me (in communism). Just to do
          my own liking, which is a purely selfish
          attitude I know but . . . I can't do anything
          to change it, 'cos if I went out in the street,
          suppose I found out I was a born leader or
          something, and went into the street, and got
          all the people to follow me, and just sort of

overthrew the government, a nice little
thing, so everything I believe in everyone's
got to live by. Well, I'm just imposing my
will on everyone else, the same as they'd
do to me. So I just dropped out, and fuck
them, I'm not happy. But I'm happier than
I was before. . . . But there again I can't
really see myself joining anything. I might
believe in what they're doing, their
overall policies, I don't think I could obey
orders that seem to be wrong, that's why I
could never join a political organization
because, uhm . . . I got this little individual
thing, my own, to worry about, you know.

It was the final tragic limit of their culture that political
activity was discredited by the hippies and seen only in this kind
of light – and not as the necessary extension of their own powers
and feelings into the realm of the struggle for the material
organization of the world. The lack of interest, or ability, here
meant that there was no hope of producing in the long term the
conditions upon which their own culture could expand and
develop. It also meant that there was a vacuum in their political
thinking, and that in its weaker forms and movements their
culture could become fatalist, quietist and jaundiced. In
contrast to the virility and air of resistance in Les's earlier
statement, should be put the pessimism, the circumscribed
sense of actual power in a confrontation, the sense of
persecution rather than revolution, the ambiguity and even
regret about what is caricatured as the conventional account of
the hippy's danger to society, in the following comments. They
were typical of a minority, but important and growing, element
in the scene. These attitudes had always been inherent, though
recessive, in the classic hippy style. These comments foreshadow
demise by a desertion of struggle, of the political:

Tony: I think what causes society to be intolerant
          is fear, they think we are going to change
          their way of life. . . . I don't think I
          represent any serious threat . . . you know,
          uhm. . . .

The hippies

Harry: Well, you don't know.
Tony: I'm in the house here twenty-three hours
           out of twenty-four.
Paul: We represent this threat to their way of life.
Ian: Yes, they think we're going to take their TVs
           and things away, and make them all live
           in filthy little bed-sitters, and communes
           and things, and rape their daughters. . . .
Paul: They won't leave us alone, it will get worse.

6 The experience of drugs

Drugs were used massively by the hippies. A survey by the local vicar showed that drug use was very common and another survey by a Church of England worker, *Spiritual Undercurrents on the Drug Scene*, unquestioningly took the hippies I have been describing as archetypal examples of drug-users. The drug squad said that the hippy culture formed the main infrastructure of contact, supply and consumption of drugs in the city. All the people with whom I taped discussion sessions were known in person to the drug squad.

Drug use was one of the central topics of conversation on the scene. There was a wide and well-used range of terms for types and sub-types of various drugs: weed, hash, Afghani, Moroccan (cannabis), acid (LSD), benny, dex, purple hearts, French blues, black bombers, amphetamines, sleepers and mandrax (barbiturates).

There was avid discussion about the effects of various drugs, and great interest taken in their supposed different properties. It was common for drug experiences to be recounted, marked over and analysed at great length. Weird or unusual experience was given particular attention. There also seemed to be a culturally appropriate way of acting out 'being stoned', and especially, of 'tripping': this included clear behavioural signs ranging from the sleepy and slightly out-of-focus look of the smoker to the disordered, disconcerting unpredictability of the acid-head.

This interest in, and dramatization of, the drug experience demonstrates but does not explain the important role of drugs in the hippy culture. It is not actually in these surface – possibly random or arbitrary – characteristics that the real importance of drugs is to be found. The essence of the dialectical role of drugs is that they supplied the raw material of open and exceptional experience which could be interpreted in appropriate social and cultural ways to reflect and develop other aspects of consciousness and activity so as to further modify the drug experience, and so on and so on.

Most basically these material and physical effects were interpreted as, and represented, a passage through a symbolic barrier: a barrier, like King Kong's wall, erected to preserve the illusion of sanity in the conventional world. The 'head' was defined not even so much by his drug use, but by his existential presence on the *other side* of this symbolic barrier – in confrontation, it seemed, with the archetypes of his own and others' unmediated experience. Appearance and location put the hippies through a material barrier against straight society. Drugs completed the cultural and experiential passage – or more precisely, provided the dialectical material lever. The symbolic passage, however, was the thing, and could be made by 'way-out' individuals even without the help of drugs, and more rarely without the help of the culture. On the other hand, those who took drugs, even where they were in the culture, and experienced no internal journey were not 'heads': they were just day-trippers in a foreign land.

As we have seen the particular form of policing adopted by the drug squad also augmented the material base of drug use available and facilitated its interpretation for a certain kind of symbolic meaning: for the dark heroism of division.

The point is, of course, that the drugs did not *intrinsically* contain a separate and alien fully-formed world. Drugs were not micro-films of experience surreptitiously slipped on to the deep projector of the mind. They were more experiential trip-switches to bring entry into a world which was essentially self and socially created: or more commonly for the same world to be seen differently and without guilt. The experience of the previous period was often, indeed, seen as a kind of blueprint for the 'acid-trip':

Val: Well, you have to prepare yourself, I mean,
              you might only have to prepare yourself,
              say, for a week or a month, twelve months,
              maybe, but it takes yogas a whole life-time,

	ten years, twenty years, a whole life-time.
Norman:	Your 'trip' consists of what you've done weeks before, and the state of your mind at that particular moment.

This is not to say that hash and acid in particular do not have definite effects on human consciousness. They do, and for the attentive the perceived change of consciousness is the basis for an existential passage – *something* has happened which demands a cultural content. The physiological basis of change could, however, be interpreted in many different *cultural* forms, and the objective chemical basis of changed consciousness does not contradict the possibility of reaching a similar state of existential awareness in non-physical ways. As Les said in one discussion:

Les:	Could be by itself [referring to experiences of heightened consciousness] or could be with acid, could be with any drug or without any drug, that's the whole point, you know, drugs give you the opportunity to change your consciousness, in other words, give you new insights. They just provide the opportunity, different people use them in different ways for different reasons, and this is what a lot of the fuck-up on the scene is about. 'Straights' use alcohol to blot out . . . to lower the level of consciousness.

Though drugs were only inverted placebos, keys to experience, rather than experience, they were still accorded a sacred place in the head culture. This was another form of their dialectical impact on the culture. A whole reverential ritual had developed around different kinds of drug use, and these produced their own material practices and material effects which further widened the dialectical sweep of drugs in the culture. The serious head smoker inhaled very much more deeply, and kept the smoke in the lungs very much longer, than did the casual user. He was also very much more likely to control the amount of the drug, during the ritualistic making of the 'joint', at a high consistent level than was the casual smoker.

The experience of drugs

There was also much more care taken to make the circumstances of smoking more conducive to bringing out the drug's full effect on consciousness and perception. In the case of acid, trips would be prepared and planned for, and supportive contexts organized, in a way quite different from the more arbitrary conditions of innocent experimentation.

The ritualistic practices, then, which grew to surround the drug both increased the 'raw' effect they had on consciousness (through greater ingestion) and resonated this experience in a particular way (through greater focusing of the circumstances of ingestion). The greater raw experience thus provided gave more scope for appropriate cultural interpretation, which in turn facilitated more intensive smoking rituals, producing higher levels of ingestion, etc., etc.

What was the particular nature of the increasing dialectical influence of drugs on consciousness? As I said, drugs were the dialectical key to the recognition of experience that had always been *immanent.* Perhaps the most characteristic element of this change was a diminished sense of personal responsibility in the world. We saw before that a central part of the hippy culture is its liberating sense of determination and loss of agency in the world. This was enormously aided by drugs because their influence could be seen as taking the responsibility for you and your state of consciousness. You could cease trying. You were released from the bars of the protestant ethic. This produced a profound sense of freedom and insight. You could relax from personal vigil. The world might hold its commonsense constructs together if it could. You would not. It was too late for that. At last, and sometimes it seemed quite suddenly, you could see into the precarious balance called reality. The drug experience prised open a particular view of the profound contradiction: man is both free and determined – neither of which was contained in the conventional 'I'.

Drugs, therefore, helped to generate the symbolic belief among the hippies, stretching far beyond the actual drug experience, that they were importantly carried by circumstance and not vice versa. Drug experience most perfectly represented and helped to produce a fundamental ontological change from the usual sense of the self as autonomous and determining, to one of the self as autonomous in a special way but also very

138

much determined. This was the essential nature of the barrier between the straight and the hip. Guilt flowed from the hippy world. It was only worth feeling guilt if it implied action to take it away: to screw up the senses for precise effort. No such action was possible. There was an utter freedom of the mind and senses in being determined: lost in the void of your own possibilities at the still centre of the dialectic. The head experienced, rode down and in, the meaning of those forces which the alert, autonomous mind – whilst still determined – nevertheless tries to block from its conscious pathways.

In a sense, then, nothing could harm the head, when 'high'. He was beyond the reach of coercion in the world. Because he had seen the ultimately coercive nature of life, and had found it liberating, nothing could touch him again. Of course, the head did not feel quite so safe when he 'came down', and the drugs bust, particularly by uniformed police, threatened to bring this whole world down, but something of these feelings remained all the time. It was even a brief understanding of this perspective which put him on the 'head' and 'freak' side of the symbolic barrier.

To the head, 'straight' consciousness was the ratio-technical encirclement of man's capacity to experience. If you could trust yourself to leave that tight circle, you were given new eyes, new ears, new skin: tuned to areas still within the mind. Drugs were seen as the way *par excellence* of unwinding the tightness of reality. Whether you liked it or not, they seemed to begin to unravel the real world. The head did like it. The 'straight' on drugs did not like it. He waited apprehensively until the threads took themselves up again.

The claimed ability of drugs, and especially acid, to open up blocked experiential areas was absolutely central to the whole culture:

Les:	You can actually see, and I have seen, music. I have seen it bubbling out of the speakers.
Val:	You see, you are *trapped* by all your senses, you're trapped by touch and smell and taste and sight and sound, but you can take acid, the cross-over, so you are no longer trapped, you are no longer trapped in the

	way you see the world.
Les:	With acid you tend towards a total experience of all the senses, particularly the visual ones. You can see other senses, I haven't seen a smell, but I have seen a sound and have heard a colour.
Les:	I have been, well, I did lay a 'chick' on acid once, and it was the most incredible experience I think I have ever had, because the whole orgasm becomes total, uhm . . . not only in the neurological centre of the brain that gives you a sensation of pleasure, not only in the tip of the penis, but over the whole of the body, man, in the tips of my fingers, I have orgasm after orgasm. Now that was a state of as near bliss that I think I shall ever get to . . . it was totally incredible and the only thing that stopped me having these orgasms was my own physical strength, energy had just drained away from my limbs. It was the most incredible experience, because I could just feel the energy draining away, I was aware my muscles were converting less oxygen . . . most incredible thing.

The head, as we saw in chapter 5, was always alive to the unusual in common situations. This owed much to the dialectical experience of drugs. Although living in the shared world, he saw more facets in it, and light refractions from it, even without drugs, than ever a straight could. The head 'gazes at', the straight 'manages' the real world.

A crucial aspect of this yielding to experience, as we also saw in chapter 5, was a total preoccupation with the 'now'. If experience is all, then presence is all. The main dimension of presence is 'nowness'. Drugs both reflected and represented this aspect of the culture, concentrated it and further produced it:

| Keith: | 'Dope' has meant a certain amount of freedom, as a result of, of . . . being much more aware of what is, you know . . . what |

is rather than what was or will be. You know
. . . uhm . . . I believe that one must live
in the present, you know, this instant,
now, experiencing now for what it is,
because it is . . . because it is for no other
reason. I suppose I could have gone into a
monastery and meditated and, perhaps,
found out the same thing in about fifty
years, I've just found out how to do it,
acids just speeded up the process of it, you
know, well, quite considerably.

This encapsulation by the 'now', and the feeling of freedom
to 'walk around and feel the moment', led to a sensed
breakdown of conventional notions of time – especially on the
trip but also in a general way:

Les: Everything is totally irrelevant [referring to
experience on a 'trip'], everything is totally
relevant and totally irrelevant.

Norman: You realize that time is man-made, there is
no such a thing as 'time', it's a load of cock,
something that man has made to
computerize himself by, so that he can
regulate—

Val: There's a time within the brain, biological
clock that paces your life at the conscious
level—

Les: That gets fucked up on acid—

Val: You think, you know, I have just done that
or I'm going to do that in a moment, you
think like that all the time, and that's time.

Norman: Yes, but that's *pure* time, but time as we
regard it normally, like 1 o'clock or 4
o'clock, that's a load of crap. I feel like
throwing my watch away.

Les: I did throw mine away.

This subjective sense of time, the maximal openness of the
senses, and the essential lack of autonomy, concentrated,

summed up and further projected in the drug experience, could dispel normal feelings of revulsion, and render objectively distasteful situations pleasurable and even fascinating:

Keith: Well, like I was with a chick and she was sick all over the floor, man, we were both sort of really spaced out, the room was swirling and I couldn't tell where I began or anything else, but I got it together to clean up the sick. I wasn't even revolted by it, and usually I am, you know, someone has only got to be sick in the same room as me normally, and I want to puke as well. But I was in there with my bare hands scooping the sick up into a bowl.

Les: They had this bog at Bath, and it must have been a football pitch long, and it was like corrugated iron bent double in V-sections, like on to the other all the way down.

Stuart: You've got to be a tall guy standing at one end.

Les: And everybody was sort of pissing, it was just people all down this thing, and I was at the small end and it was like a fucking river, I was 'tripping' like fuck, and it was beautiful, you know, I got really hung up on the piss.

Stuart: All the dog-ends and matches floating down.

Les: It was beautiful, the stink was fucking terrible.

In certain respects the hippy involvement with drugs and the dialectical effects it produced in their experience, culture and consciousness comprised a classic faith paradox. This was another aspect of the barrier between the straight and the hip. Either you understood or you did not. There was no question of rational proof. The kind of questions which might occur to outsiders become irrelevant inside. To ask certain questions was to show that the answer could never be appreciated.

This 'catch 22' aspect of the drug culture was a source of particular confusion to well-meaning agencies and sympathetic groups. A concern with 'causes', their isolation, and ultimately, their modification, as in the usual notion of the causal escalation from soft to hard drugs, is the basis for the vast majority of attempts to understand drug cultures. They all aim at making the drug-user reassert his own autonomy within the causal chain. These approaches simply never meet the real terms of the drug experience. For the head, it was precisely *lack* of autonomy which made him most free to experience the full richness of consciousness. Expanded awareness could overview *normal* consciousness as one corner of its map. Exhortations for a return to this country merely confirm the head's new mapping of experience.

Within their respective subjective terms, the drug-user knows the social worker much better than the social worker knows him. The point of greatest divergence between the 'objective', causal, welfare perspective, and the internal experience of a ꞊rug culture, is located in contradictory notions of freedom. For welfare workers freedom is self-responsibility. For the head freedom is existential *lack* of responsibility. The head's sense of freedom, though, unlike the welfare one, is not open to reasonable discussion. It *is* an existential experience, not a logical construct.

This sense of 'faith understanding', fed, and was fed by, all other aspects of the hippy culture. They were very impatient with causal and outside explanations. They wanted the experience of a thing and were bored by what they took to be the shell of experience-explanation.

This sense of faith and direct experiential appropriation of complex matters, in relation to the other intensities of their culture, led easily into forms of mystical experience. As we saw in chapter 5 one of the absolutely central preoccupations of the head culture was the continual pressure towards keeping their spiritual life engaged. Drugs provided one of the most sustainable contacts with this part of their experience, and kept its feeling alive in other parts of the culture which in their turn influenced the drug experience. It was in the mystical experience that the individual felt himself irrevocably put beyond the reach of the everyday world and its insistence on autonomy. If you were part of the cosmic consciousness, part of God, in fact you *were* God, then notions of causation and personal autonomy were simply misunderstandings. All aspects of life were part of you, so how could you war against yourself?

There was a direct contact here, of course, with what the heads understood of Eastern religion and culture. Only rarely, however, was there a really detailed knowledge of these religions. The East was taken more as a metaphor for their position than as a grammar for marking it out. The easy use of the reference should not disguise the desperate authenticity and importance of the experience beneath:

Les:	I believe there is a godhead and I believe in the pure energy of life which I've found out a lot about on acid, it was a tremendously religious thing with me at one time.
Stuart:	Yes, but do you believe there is a figurehead?
Les:	Yeah, where my head is now I take it as my Bible, the I-ching, or whatever you would like to call it, the Chinese book of changes. . . . I believe when I go through the book of changes, and I see the Hexagram, the changes shown to me. Now not only do I try to live my life along these lines at that particular moment, but I believe that what I am doing according to the book of changes and according to my own views of humanity and according to my concepts of the godhead, the pure energy life-force, this is gonna make things better for other people, the people that surround me immediately, the people that I know. My debt to society, if you want to put it that way, that the things I owe my fellow man, I owe myself.
Les:	Yeah, because the Eastern concepts of religion have a lot in common with acid, or the acid concepts of religion.
Val:	The West takes the view that God is a

transcendental being, in other words he's separate from the world, and you enter into the kingdom of heaven if you've been a good man in this life [laughter].

And, you know, you may become one with God, but the East takes the view that God is immanent and we are God in God, you know, God is in us, and this is what acid gives you.

Norman: That's I think . . . one of the most blissful moments . . . if you want to . . . the knowledge . . . that . . . you're God.

The drug experience resonated with and helped to form many other practices and experiences in the hippy culture. It was widely believed that drugs greatly helped in the appreciation of music. It was often claimed of groups like Frank Zappa, Jimi Hendrix and Pink Floyd, that their music could not be understood without the use of drugs, and was beyond the comprehension of 'straights' for this very reason. Different drug experiences had different properties as a mediation of musical response. There was a hierarchy of drugs in terms of their influence on musical appreciation, acid was the strongest drug in common use and produced the most profound changes:

Les: These guys are turned on you know, half of what he says doesn't mean fuck all to anybody who isn't turned on, it really doesn't. Look at the Stones, you listen to the Stones tripping, and wow that's something entirely different again.

Tony: I think that if you smoke this enables you to sit back and relax more than anything, and let's you listen, you know, without any hang-ups, you sit back and listen. Whereas with acid, you see right into the music, it's a bigger thing altogether.

Tony: I think the Floyd must be . . . you hear things on Floyd on acid, well I do, that I don't hear when I'm straight.

145

PW:	You hear things that you don't normally?
Norman:	It's like, you hear, say, part of a new record, you listen to it when you've had nothing, and listen to it again when you've taken acid, and it's totally different, you hear, pick up, different things from what you've heard before.
Roger:	A good example is Tyrannosaurus Rex, if you listened to them, and you'd never tripped you wouldn't have a clue about what they're singing about, but after you'd tripped and listened to them, you'd actually understand some of what they're singing about.
PW:	Is it ever possible for a 'straight' to understand?
Tony:	Yeah, they can probably listen to it like we can listen to *Top of the Pops*, they're probably listening to it, but they're not actually getting right into it, you know, they're just listening to it pleasantly.

It was also widely believed that their preferred musicians composed and performed their music under the influence of drugs, and that after the experience of drugs, one could see changes in the music itself reflecting the musical group's move from one drug to another:

Stuart:	The Beatles, for me, were smoking a long time before they made it, yet there's definitely a line in the music where they changed from smoke to acid.
Les:	Yea, 'Lucy In The Sky With Diamonds', man, that was the sort of. . . .
Stuart:	Well, now, *Revolver*, you could say, because there was 'Strawberry Fields Forever' . . . that was the real turning-point when they put out that simple. . . . 'Strawberry Fields', was the first one where they changed from smoke to acid . . . you could definitely see it.

A further common assertion was that drugs 'lengthened time' and 'spaced out' the music. The drug experience here clearly synthesized with other really central elements of the culture, and further reflected and developed them in a dialectical relationship with music:

Les: Your perception becomes far more intensified, and intellectual perception as well as the pure sort of pleasure in the head.

Stuart: If you've been on some very good smoke, and you're really out of your head, these, especially the LPs that are out now, where there's sort of half an LP, or an LP of just one record, time becomes completely irrelevant, not only irrelevant, it just becomes nothing . . . you can get into the music that much, that time . . . irrelevant is the wrong word for it, it just becomes non-existent. Once you got into it, if somebody should switch it off, and say 'How long has that record been playing?', you wouldn't be able to say it's been playing ten minutes, two minutes, five minutes, a week.

John: It sort of kills the time, it kills the time stone dead, you don't sort of sit and think, this is a great solo or anything, you sort of live in every second, don't you, while it's playing. When it finishes, you're surprised, you know.

We can see the relevance here of a common phrase used by the hippies to denote experiences on drugs – 'spaced out'. In the space held open by the drug experience they said that it was possible to follow the line of particular instruments, and to differentiate the sound of different instruments in a way that was impossible normally, and to feel actually *in* the music. Les even said that he sometimes felt that *he was* the music.

Some of the hippies said that they had experienced synesthesia listening to music on a 'trip'. We can see this is an extreme version of the search for experiential density applied to

147

musical experience. It is as if the precise nature of the music was concentrated upon so intensely that the individual had gone right through the phenomenal surface into new dimensions where the music registered on more than one sense. Music was seen 'bubbling out of speakers', and different notes came out as different colours. We see here the most extreme form of the penetration and reworking of the 'natural' to yield a fuller and even more experiential, psychedelic version of nature: an even more riveting kaleidoscope of the 'now'.

There was also a double conjunction and reciprocal development of meaning in the culture between drug and musical experience in the area of mystical experience. Music – and often carefully selected individual tracks or albums – listened to under the influence of drugs, could, it seems, definitely encourage or strengthen the mystical feelings experienced sometimes on a trip. As we shall see in chapter 7 music itself was trusted because the undecipherability of its code protected the feelings it expressed from philistine disbelief. Music, in conjunction with drugs and mediated through drugs, in some way made the cold eye of logic doubly remote. The lag made spiritual heightening more prolonged and self-convincing.

If there is a danger at this point of losing sight of the conventional perspective, we should remember that many of the states, feelings and actions described in this chapter were conventionally seen as pathological. If the hippies used stylistic psychotic sub-plots to express their identity in half-mockery of this perspective, it is also true that there *was* a high rate of breakdown and suicide in their culture. The careful uncovering of the rest of their experience and culture should not minimize the tragic fact that this experience could be unstable and poorly grounded – especially when exposed to the real world and its sceptical institutions. The drug squad attest this sombre fact in their own tangential, contradictory way:

B: Very often we will talk to a kid on the drug scene, and he's talking about drugs, and we suddenly realize that it's not drugs that are affecting this kid. It's something much more deep-rooted and we refer many of them to

hospital. And this has been found at the
hospital that, although they've been hiding
behind drugs, they have had a psychiatric
illness, not a severe one. You can get a kid
who says 'I'm addicted to pot, you know'.
Some doctors would think it so-called
cannabis psychosis, but I know that, uhm,
the way certain doctors operate is this: if they
get a person come into them, if he's been
referred by, and from other referrals, they
will forget drugs entirely and start
examining as a psychiatric patient, and they
will probably find somewhere along the line,
that he has got some slight psychiatric
disorder, you know, he would be a
schizophrenic or. . . .

The status of experience and the value of cultural production
and insight are difficult to weigh against individual failure and
disorientation. Certainly I would argue that we should not see
drug use, in a general way, as necessarily pathological.
Certainly, for instance, we should understand the conventional
definitions in relation to the way in which the
'professionalization' and standardization of behavioural
psychiatry has branded any unusual experience as 'sick', and
lends itself so easily for use in social control. In the face of a
hostile and repressive social order the hippies at least had the
courage to explore what they saw as the totality of their
existence.

The notion of pathology does, however, bring up much more
acutely the question of the particular chemical effects of
different drugs and their interaction with cultural meanings.
The analysis so far might suggest that the range of cultural
interpretation and moulding of drug experience is limitless. The
insistence on the external and social origin of the basic meanings
surrounding drug use in opposition to a simple notion of
pathology has perhaps minimized the role of certain important
effects and the associated limits of the various drugs. Drugs do
supply potent experience which, even if polyvalent and

appropriated finally in cultural ways, is nevertheless quite real and sometimes devastating. Not only is it real, but it sets the outer limits for interpretation. It may not determine the cultural meaning and effect within the area it designates as 'open', but outside this it prevents all interpretation. The drug experience must be seen as a limiting as well as an enabling resource for cultural interpretation. This was the basis of what might be thought of as a cultural pharmacology of drugs on the head scene – the sense among the heads of the different social possibilities associated with different drugs – a sense ultimately based on their chemical nature.

Hash was the common denominator of all drugs, and was the most commonly used and most bland in its effects. It was recognized that many other groups used the drug in quite different ways, with quite different meanings. It was perfectly possible to use the drug on the 'straight' scene without any 'hip' connotations at all. Acid was seen as a much more powerful drug altogether and, because of its more direct effect on consciousness, a much more culturally positive drug. It was felt that 'straights' were likely to take the drug only once and then be 'frightened off'. Many hippies were themselves frightened of the drug. They were not necessarily out-group figures since they were likely to be part of the wider symbolic hippy world and so understood, *at some level*, what it was like to trip, but they were unlikely to be seen as 'real' heads. The 'real' heads, however, did not use acid indiscriminately. They used it regularly and carefully, preparing themselves and their environment quite meticulously for the experience, or finely spotting the mood in which acid would go well. Bad trips, dissociation and disorientation – and the disasters which sometimes followed – came from ignoring these only too well-known ground rules.

Heroin was as much beyond acid as acid was beyond hash, but in a less culturally appropriate manner. It had, as it were, only a one-way dialectical relationship with the culture. The 'dangers' of H were well recognized and its effects were seen as harder to control than those of other drugs.

According to the drug squad the level of drug addiction in the city had fallen right down to single figures from the scores registered in the mid-1960s. But heroin was a drug that was not talked about too much on the scene. If you were using it even occasionally, only your closest associates would know. It was also believed that dependency could be avoided by careful and occasional 'skin popping' rather than 'mainlining'.[2] Although its power was known, the drug was not subject to the mystification and fear which surrounds its supposed effects in conventional society. For the head it was seen as a powerful agency which must be treated with care rather than as an evil force: normally to be avoided, it could be welcomed in desperate circumstances.

The cultural meaning of 'mainlining' H among the hippies seemed mainly to be in a symbolic extension of its supposed physical irreversibility. The passage on heroin was not simply through a symbolic barrier as with other drugs. It was an unanswerable closure. You could not be any further out, you could not be more prey to external determination. You could not give up more of your own autonomy. You had burnt your boats and could not return. In one way this made H the supreme expression of drug-culture meanings. It held writ large and indelibly, all those things that separated the 'head' from the gauche mundanenessd of 'straight' life. It was an expression of loyalty to beyond-the-barrier meanings that the straight could never begin to understand, and which straight society could never bring you back from. On the other hand, in an indirect admission of the supremacy of symbolic states over real ones, and for us, clear evidence that the heroin drug experience could not be influenced and moulded as could that of acid or hash, H was partly distrusted. Its force demanded respect. Its secret meanings could be the last ones you would know. There was an unanswerable-anti-straight-supremely-hip ambience about the drug but also a sense of closure, of giving up, of death. Its play of meaning could not be brought further back into life. In this sense we see a very clear limitation of cultural meaning set by the pharmacological base of a drug.

The role of amphetamines and barbiturates seemed to be rather outside of the mainstream. They were not central to the head scene in the way that dope and acid were. They were usually associated more with other cultural groups. In the hippy scene they seemed to be used more on an *ad hoc* basis, to stay awake to allow the completion of some task or another or to be certain of sleep when rest was required. There was the question of supply, of course, and where nothing else was available pills would be taken. In a drug culture with strong symbolic structures, all drugs are seen as valuable, and any drug is capable of giving some appropriate effects.

The point of this chapter has been to suggest that drug experience can be understood at a cultural level, and that in real cultures they are included in dialectical processes which are dynamic and creative. They both hold and develop certain profound meanings for the head.

This is not an argument for dismissing the chemical effect of drugs on the human organism. They set the outer limits and supply the raw experience for induction into cultural forms. Even at this level, however, we should recognize that the culture is able *usually* to control this objective basis of its experience to a large extent. Where control is minimal, use is minimal. Drugs do not enforce a one-way inner coded determination of sickness and suffering: they do not lie along a simple scale of automatic escalation. They are held in distinctive cultural processes: the act of human appropriation – within the limits set by the drugs – is what gives them their specific meaning in society. Removal or prohibition of drugs would not remove the force of meanings which need expression. They may find other, more treacherous objects.

7 The creative age

Those big riffs on the guitar, sums up a lot.

Tony on Jimi Hendrix

In sheer quantitative terms, there was a massive interaction between a certain kind of pop music and the hippy culture. It is hard to conceive of the hippy without linking him to a certain kind of 'progressive' pop music. It is a relationship which could be arbitrary or random as duly recorded, in their customary manner, by the city drug squad. It is interesting that Benny (a good friend of Les and Stuart) reportedly penetrates this surface response and urges a fuller awareness of a complex cultural relationship.

A: Well, of course, they sit down during most of the day doing nothing, so they've got to have some form of entertainment; they must take an interest in something and, of course, they do take an interest in music; we've spent whole nights in the Lafayette talking about music.

It's just part of the conversation; we've talked about everything from Canadian mythology, to Greek mythology, as well as music. We've had arguments over what is music. I remember one night Benny said to us: 'You see, you don't know what music is, mister, you've no idea what music is.' I said: 'Well, whats good to you might not be good to me, you see. . . . I mean, after all it's just something that gets hold of you.'

The hippy's relation to his music was not arbitrary. It was not just a case of happening to leave the radio or television on and, besides, there was little of their music on the popular channels. Nor was their musical interest a case of seizing anything of unusual interest out of boredom or a desire for startling conversation pieces. They deliberately chose their musical environment – post *Sergeant Pepper*, 'progressive' music – and went to great lengths to preserve it and to exclude Top twenty and commercial music.

Only specific kinds of music were chosen because they – and not others – were able to hold, develop and return those meanings and experiences which were important in the hippy culture.

The hippies' profound distinction, for instance, between the authentic and the non-authentic was reflected in certain objective features of their music. All critics agree that the most distinctive features of the 'progressive' music of the middle and late 1960s was its creativity and originality:[1]

> If you want to come up with a singular, most important trend in this new music, I think it has to be something like: it is original, composed by the people who perform it, created by them – even if they have to fight the record companies to do it – so that it is really a creative action and not a commercial pile of shit thrown together by business people who think they know what John Doe and Mr Jones really want. (Frank Zappa)

The early 1960s was a period of stagnation in pop music. The exciting advances of the 1950s had ground to a halt. The commercial influence had been to hold to the *status quo* as long as possible. There were no reliable market forecasting techniques in this industry, as there were in other consumer areas, and there was no will to provide 'risk' capital unless it was really necessary or a return guaranteed. The only feasible method of prediction was extrapolation, or the use of smoothed averages. In essence this meant following the trend of what had gone previously: wiping the indicators that lay too far from the main trend. This kind of commercial determination tended to make music inauthentic, lifeless and repetitious. In the early 1960s all pop music was made in this kind of commercial nexus.

The Beatles, in particular, helped to break this cycle of

commercial determination. They were the first pop group of the 1960s to express something of themselves, and their artistic feelings, directly. A string of commercial successes following 'Love Me Do' in 1962 strengthened their arm against the imperatives of the old system. The period before *Sergeant Pepper* saw such tracks as 'Eleanor Rigby', 'Strawberry Fields', showing clear development in imaginative scope and technique from the earlier 'Love Me Do', and 'Please Please Me'. And the music had awoken tastes in at least part of the market which could not now be ignored. People were not buying *any* consumer package, but the Beatles. This gave them an unprecedented opportunity to produce music more securely based on their own creative authenticity.

There still remained a large conventional market and this could be fed with the old formulae, but the newly created and growing market was much more selective. What was most worrying to the commercial interests was that they did not know this market nor could they understand the music. It was only the new 'reliable' product groups who could do any kind of 'forecasting' or 'mixing'. For a strange, brief period creative authenticity and the purities of consumer marketing coincided. Select groups were simply allowed to get on with it. The Beatles were inevitably the first to produce something which was bold, original and successful: *Sergeant Pepper's Lonely Hearts Club Band*. The record made a lot of money but it was in no sense simply commercially determined. It was mainly determined by the Beatles' own creative imagination. Its success showed that the Beatles' aesthetic was buried in an age. They had pioneered an important, nodal break from the dead hand of commercial determination. Many groups followed through the breach to form what became known as 'the underground' and further develop what was seen as 'progressive music'.

We can see, therefore, that the hippies' general notion of authenticity had a reflection in the real dimensions of their preferred music. This principle was socially activated time and again in critical opinion. Groups who were not even particularly liked in musical terms were given an automatic respect if they were 'doing their own thing'.

An interest in LPs rather than in singles was another of the fundamental characteristics of the hippies' relation to music:

Les:	I just don't know anybody that's got a 45 record, has anyone got a 45?
Sue:	Yeah, 'Coming Home'.
Stuart:	Oh yeah, I've got one I think, but I nicked it.

We must understand this, again, in terms of the particular role music played in the lives of the hippies. Music was serious for them and not a matter of momentary diversion. The appropriate way to receive music was, therefore, in quiet concentrated listening. Music was not simple enjoyment, a distraction, it was an *experience*. The LP form is clearly more suited to these demands than is the single.

The 'concept album' held a particular relevance for the hippies. Until the time of the Beatles the LP was used, either as a collection of the greatest hits, or as an outlet for singles with poor commercial prospects. But undergound music utilized the LP form for the first time as a musical resource by using its full length for unitary and thematic productions. One song could take up a whole track and in the Grateful Dead's *Live Dead* one composition takes up three album sides. Albums were thematic and meant to be listened to as a whole in one sitting. Celebrated 'concept' albums such as the Beatles' *Sergeant Pepper's Lonely Hearts Club Band*, *Days of Future Past*, by the Moody Blues, *Tommy* by the Who, and *Blows Against the Empire* by Paul Kantner, were meant to be taken as a whole experience in one sitting. LPs of this type were clearly for *listening to*. They were to be trusted for themselves to stretch through a whole mood without doubt or impatience leading to an early rejection – as it would have done in the motor-bike culture, for instance.

The hippies responded fully to, and aspects of their culture were developed by, the new possibilities in the concept album form. For them a single was too short. It was riveted to a limited feeling. It was unable to contain the sweep of real experience: experience which could be represented by the new possibilities of the concept album.

Another important aspect of the role of the music in the culture was the relative unimportance of dance. As we have seen, little of the hippy's general identity was expressed through autonomous bodily movement, so there was no demand that the music should parallel rhythmic bodily movement in a regular clear beat or encourage dancing. Beat was not a way of encouraging and reflecting physical action, but a way of demanding attention in the head. The heavy asymmetric beat of Hendrix or Zappa was appreciated but not for the encouragement to dance it supplied. It was its penetrating, expressive nature which was valued. It was not the body, but the consciousness which could not ignore it. Nor was the music played loud – as it often was – to emphasize dance beat. This was done to enlarge the experience of the listener to the point of vibrating his ribcage as well as his eardrums, and to repress all other stimuli. Dancing grace for itself was rarely remarked upon. Where dance did attract attention it was because it was 'freaky' and unusual: a kind of 'mad' style bizarrely expressing meanings in the head.

Song words had much more importance for, and were more closely scrutinized by, the hippies than was the case for instance with the bikeboys. Their music clearly reflected and developed this interest.

The period of the change from 'teeny bopper' music to 'underground' music saw a massive and widely documented change in the nature of lyrics. The career of the Beatles illustrates this well. In their first four LPs, of 55 songs only 8 were not concerned with love and courtship relations. In *Sergeant Pepper*, the lyrics covered a much wider range. There were four tracks concerning drugs, one track concerning Eastern mysticism, and one track, 'A Day In The Life', made an impressive, if mysterious, statement about the nature of modern urban experience. Later albums confirmed and widened this development. On the double albums, only 7 out of 28 tracks, and on *Abbey Road*, only 3 out of 16 tracks, were concerned with love or emotional relationships. The quality of lyrics was also given a huge impetus forward by Bob Dylan. He developed a laconic, enigmatic but telling half-statement, and a surrealist style which expressed real insight into the alienation and tensions of modern America. Lyrics, as well as the music, demanded serious listening and attention. The hippies were prepared to give it, and have it further encouraged.

In more internal ways the hippies preferred music that was answerable to, and helped to further develop, important aspects

157

of their culture. The creative questioning and irreverent mockery of normal social conventions and attitudes by the hippies was reflected by the musical inventiveness of the 'progressive' groups. 'Progressive' music experimented with, and made musical resources out of, what were the limitations, or accepted conventions – such as the LP – the music world. 'Way-out' musical style, exploiting a variety of sound-effects, was the musical equivalent of their own unpredictable, 'way-out' social style. Loudness itself was exploited. The Rolling Stones' record 'Let It Bleed', carried the imperative, 'This record must be played loud'. Led Zeppelin in a 'Whole Lot Of Love' used the contrast of silence and great noise to make dramatic points. Tim Souster in a talk for Radio 3 (27 May 1970) analysed the implications of working at a high volume, and the ways in which they have been *used* as resources rather than as simply imposing limits:

> An organ solo such as that one ['Hope For Happiness', Soft Machine], with its unbroken melody line, is determined by the nature of the electric organ. When working at a very high volume, one can't take one's fingers from the keyboards for fear of accoustical feedback between the instrument and the loudspeakers. One solution to this problem is the long melodic lines and the unbroken fast passage work we have just heard. It seems to me that it is this situation, where a new music fits a new instrument, that we find pop music breaking new ground in a way impossible in any other medium. Here volume has become a musical resource.

Epps adds an important point about the creative use of feedback in the same broadcast:

> Although it's normally regarded as the curse of electric instruments, feedback has been integrated into the very different styles of Pete Townshend and Jimi Hendrix and, most radically, of Lou Reed the lead guitarist and singer of the New York group, the Velvet Underground. Lou Reed's solo on 'I Heard Her Call My Name' will give you an idea of the groups. Listen to the way the points at which high-pitched feedback is used are carefully judged either for melodic or dramatic effect. Here's another resource which could only have evolved in the pop medium.

A note may be added to this that the music of the Velvet Underground was widely regarded as 'H-music' by the hippies. This may well be connected with the massive alarming/exciting use made of feedback and other techniques in their music.

Other technical aids developed or creatively exploited by the 'progressive groups' included: the fuzz-box; the wah-wah pedal; multi-track tape-recorders; playing of tapes backwards; electronic synthesizers to mock up human noises such as the weird electronic screaming in the Pink Floyd's 'Careful With That Axe, Eugene'; odd and unusual shouts and laughter, such as the cold laugh at the end of George Harrison's 'Within You, Without You'. Live performances were also accompanied by complex light shows involving numerous projectors, motion-picture films, slides, strobes and colour wheels. The underground groups also exploited stereo equipment in an unusual way, switching sounds from one speaker to the other and juggling sounds between speakers. Pink Floyd are the pre-eminent English group to exploit the electronic aids in making music. In concert they are more like engineers than musicians, sitting at great consoles turning knobs and flicking switches rather than actually playing instruments.

The originality and complexity of 'progressive' music not only matched the intricacy and inventiveness of the hippy life-style, but the unusual, bizarre and exotic sounds it made possible matched and developed the 'head'-centred nature of the hippy culture, and the general emphasis on expanded awareness. The asymmetry of rhythms and unexpected developments of form in Van Morrison, the outlandish use of sound-effects by Frank Zappa, made a simple dancing-to-the-beat impossible, but allowed an almost infinite arrangements of abstract sets in the head. Top Twenty music was boring and predictable to the hippies precisely because it contained so little content, so few and impoverished counters to correlate with their own elaborate, complex meanings. The elements of surprise, contradiction and uncertainty in their music – the elements which made it almost threatening to the 'straight' listener – were precisely the elements that were prized by the hippies. They *wanted* conventional meaning to be undercut, *wanted* to be surprised and made uncertain. The common call for clarity in pop music was quite foreign to them.

It was the very lack of clarity – the multi-codedness – of their preferred music which allowed it to suggest a multitude of suggestive meanings.

In particular their music was trusted because its complexity and difficulty held logocentric meaning at bay and suggested something of their spiritual meanings without clarifying them in a way which was bound to reduce them. Instead of 'meaning' was a rich ambiguity which held sufficient points, gestures and clues to hold interpretations of divinity for a group already poised in that direction. The exhilaration produced occasionally by the music gave credence to some kind of general belief in transcendence as well as implying the impossibility of realizing it directly in normal life.

Music is anyway beyond the conventions of critical language. Underground music took this inherent quality and developed it in its own distinctive and paradoxical way with the new electronic techniques. The words, the music and the general ambience of progressive pop were often explicitly directed against conventional meaning.

Richard Meltzer, in his aesthetics of rock,[2] makes the central point:

> Bob Dylan's greatest dive into the rock 'n' roll domain, 'Like A Rolling Stone', represents an attempt to free man by rescuing him from meaning, rather than free man through meaning. John Lennon's two collections of writings have shown his desire to denigrate all meaning and thus throw intentional ambiguity into all domains of meaning.

For the hippies this lack of 'meaning' prevented exposure of, or attack on, the privileged meanings and feelings they derived from the music within the tight circle of their own culture. This kind of relation to the music also encouraged a sense of esotericism and of élitism. They had a music which only they could appreciate. This was doubly satisfying because it outraged society, as well as containing and protecting their own innermost concerns.

The suggestiveness and rich ambiguity was often sustained in the words of progressive music. The flux was maintained by innuendo, oblique reference and allusion – the brief bench-markings of a greater experience, which a ready consciousness could take subjectively, for a moment, as the whole experience.

Van Morrison's 'Madam George' (*Astral Weeks*), for example, a great favourite among the hippies, held a tight line between disintegration of meaning, and a suggestion of the 'beyond'. Many critics have suggested that this track is one of the most powerful, evocative and profound compositions in modern pop. According to the hippies it was 'beyond words', 'just incredible'. In the words of this song nostalgia was stretched through mood into something like contemplation aided by the hypnotic trance-like quality of Van Morrison's voice singing chords rather than notes. There was no incoherence, but nor was there clear meaning. The scenario could have been that of an Irish woman in a bar, but it could have been much more. The words were drenched in piquant connotations of mystical resignation. Here we run up against the pretentious. The point is that it was the very ambiguity I am trying to interpret which allowed the hippies to take their own version of the experience unguardedly.

In chapter 6 we saw that drugs and music were intimately related in the hippy culture. Many of the innovations and new techniques in their preferred music really did provide elements which allowed the expression and return of central drug-related meanings. There was something in the music – an extra, exotic, outrageous range – that was open to an esoteric coding, to be broken only by the hippies with their expanded consciousness when high or tripping. The most successful had a strange alluring seductive character of their own. In Jefferson Airplane's 'White Rabbit', for instance, one of the most celebrated drug songs ever, the words draw on connotations from *Alice in Wonderland* and evoke a powerful sense of the mystery, compulsion and inevitability of the acid-trip. The music mounts sternly to a reverberating orgasm as the dormouse's advice is repeated 'Feed your head, feed your head, feed your head'. This is an unmistakable injunction for the listener to join the singer on her trip. The surreal transplantation of the innocent phrase from a children's book, and its surprising transformation in meaning, parallels and evokes the sudden disjointing of the real world and its innocence as experience on the acid-trip:

One pill makes you larger
And one pill makes you small.
And the ones that mother gives you
Don't do anything at all.
Go ask Alice
When she's ten feet tall.

And if you go chasing rabbits
And you know you're going to fall.
Tell 'em a hookah smoking caterpillar
Has given you the call.
Call Alice
When she was just small.

When men on the chess board
Get up and tell you where to go.
And you've just had some kind of mushroom
And your mind is moving low.
Go ask Alice
I think she'll know.

When logic and proportion
Have fallen sloppy dead,
And the White Knight is talking backwards
And the Red Queen's lost her head,
Remember what the Dormouse said:
'Feed your head,
Feed your head,
Feed your head.'

There was evidence of an important effect of the music on
certain basic attitudes and their confirmation. The hippies'
tastes and attitudes were much less preformed than, say, those
of the motor-bike boys. There had been dissatisfaction and
disillusion in 'straight' life, but it was in relation to others, and
in relation to the artefacts of the culture, that clearly articulated
attitudes were fully developed. The experience of music seemed
to be an important part of this process:

Harry: It (pop music) played a big part in making
                me the way I am now. . . .

Brian: The music's got a lot to do with holding people to this sort of life. I mean, you've only got to go to the festivals, a few people are dead 'straight', but you can really enjoy yourself, it gives you a sort of insight into the sort of people, groups like, if you go and see a Floyd concert. I mean, sort of six out of ten people there are on acid, it's really lovely, you know, it gives you an insight into people.

John: The music's dangerous, I think it becomes something and you start to think, which doesn't suit the government, the leaders . . . it's dangerous because it makes people look at themselves and look around and see exactly how they're being suppressed . . . and yet it's dangerous to the point that . . . take the guy the guy down the road, Les [of this study], now Zappa fucked Les up, at least his parents would believe that. I really believe it was Zappa because he used to be a hard-working office type, and his whole life completely changed, completely changed, it got to the state where he used to come home, take off his office clothes, and put on trousers carefully patched, looked as though he had worn them every day of his life, and now he does wear them every day of his life. I think it's made him realize how futile everything is, or was, for him.

Sue: It changes your life, it changes your outlook on life, music is a development, it's a development of life . . . it changes your social habits.

Tony: Dylan's played the biggest part in most people's lives, you know, turning them on to social injustice, you know, you get sick of reading the newspapers because it's a load of crap and all of a sudden you hear this guy

> singing about things you didn't know was
> happening, start listening, sort of builds up
> from there, you know. Like an example is,
> you know, like 'Needle Of Death', you
> know, we all know about that, you know,
> somebody who didn't and they listened to
> it, you know, it's so easy to understand, you
> don't need anything to just listen to it, you
> know what it's about then.

The music also seemed to be capable of influencing feeling and emotion. People who were depressed or in a period of personal crisis often turned their attention massively to music. One of the really characteristic things about these periods was withdrawal from the community. But where people could not help, 'sounds' often could. They seemed to take over and express disorganized feeling in a way that was impossible in words. The music itself partly shaped the form of the emotion, so that in accounts afterwards of 'strange' or 'depressed' episodes, music would figure prominently, and would be used as a way of explaining what happened. Occasionally people would say that a certain track had 'made them understand', had 'changed them'. Some even argued that without some personal unhappiness certain heavy music was never 'got into'. Someone on the scene who had recently attempted to commit suicide told me that during the 'bad times' he had really 'got into Zappa', and felt he knew what the group was 'trying to do now'. This was not small-talk.

Of course, the depth and power of the relationship we are analysing between music and culture owed much to the real material dialectic between the two. The hippies were able, not only to select, but to make some direct changes in the internal form of the music. The hippy case contrasts with that of the motor-bike culture. Unlike the motor-bike boys who could only select from what was provided, the hippies, or people very like them, *could* exert a powerful influence on their music. We saw before that the crucial characteristic of 'progressive pop' during the great creative age of the late 1960s was that the performers, not the controllers, were able to decide on the artistic content of the music. Now these performers very often came from some version of the hippy culture. The music, therefore, came to reflect and develop more and more closely the concerns of this cultural group. The general hippy culture exerted a determining effect on the music just as the music exerted an effect on the culture. There was enormous potential for dialectical development. The culture contained the creative base of its own music. Many of the hippies I spoke to knew famous pop groups, or had met them, or expected to meet them in familiar cultural haunts. The media high-priest of the progressive pop movement, John Peel, was seen as quite available and from them. Through these kinds of mediations, the music really was expressing their concerns:

John: It's association, we associate ourselves with Van Morrison, we wouldn't be in the slightest surprised now if he came down, walked in the room and got a joint together.

Bob: I believe that he interprets life the same as I do.

Les: The bands that are producing music today are coming out of this life-style, they are only projecting what we are thinking. They are coming from this life-style, they are growing from us, and they are communicating what we already know.

Les: Because one identifies with it [the music], because the people that play the music we like, are us.

Norman: They're just bodies with names attached to them . . . they're just the same.

Val: They are us.

Norman: They're the same, we're one you see.

We must recognize the hippy achievement in developing such a close and resonant relationship between music and a social group. It holds many lessons. Certainly the music must not be written off as 'mad' or as the insubstantial candyfloss product of cynical commercial manipulation. Though this and other pop music is produced under capitalism as a commodity, there is a 'profane' power among minority and oppressed groups to sometimes take as their own, select and creatively develop particular artefacts to express their own meanings. The determining system of commercial interests, and the limited imagination of the dominant order, *can* be transcended at the level of living day to day relationships. The trivia which trap us can be turned against what lies behind them.

A post-script[4]

A musicological account of 'progressive' music is necessary for a satisfactory analysis. The case for the dialectic I have presented rests finally on an unequivocal comparative demonstration of the internal, technically defined, elements of 'progressive' pop and their capacity to hold certain kinds of social meaning. The general lines of such an analysis can be suggested.

'Progressive' pop has developed its own distinctive, internal structure and the possibilities it supplies for social interpretation through an exploitation of the regressive and primitivistic moment introduced by earlier rock 'n' roll. We must never be in doubt that 'progressive' music followed rock 'n' roll, and that it could not have been any other way. We can see rock 'n' roll as a deconstruction and 'progressive' music as a reconstruction. The simple expedient of replacing tonality with beat as its main organizing structure let rock 'n' roll out of the constrictions of received music. It went no further, itself, however, than a primitivistic celebration of the simplicity and timelessness it had rediscovered. The crucial simultaneous development of advanced techniques for recording and reproduction also relieved rock 'n' roll of the constriction of a transposed notation. Progressive music would have been impossible without this stage of regression, and clearing of received convention. Though this risks minimization and ignores its crucial modernity, one way of conceptualizing rock 'n' roll, and its relation to 'progressive' music, is to see it as a retracement back through the complex roots of romantic and classical music to a point where the tonal conventions had not become determining and to a point where the body was still openly in the music as beat. 'Progressive' music can be seen as an experimentation with alternative routes – exploiting the new techniques, of course – from this point into a greater complexity.

In terms of rhythm and the time-structure of music, 'progressive' pop has held to the basic inspiration pioneered by early rock 'n' roll. It has subverted the bar form by ignoring the conventional strict hierarchy of beats in the bar. In this way it has transformed the conventional rhythm of music into something much more like a continuous pulse which can suggest timelessness and random organization. However, whereas with rock 'n' roll the pulse is maintained by a simple regular beat implying timelessness through constancy or the *lack* of discontinuities, 'progressive' music has a floating varied pulse which while preserving the sense of timelessness also suggests nevertheless a kind of structure. Because of the inhibition of the temporal dimension this must be perceived in terms of a lateral, spatial extension. Here one thinks of the multiplicity of rhythms working over each other in Jimi Hendrix (for instance, 'Band Of Gypsies'), and the variations and contradictions of rhythm in Frank Zappa (for instance, 'King Kong Variations'). Electronic techniques, in particular, such as echo, feedback, stereo, loudness itself, distortion, have been used to give the impression of space and lateral extension.

In terms of its tonal structure also 'progressive' pop is similar to rock 'n' roll in overthrowing harmony as its basic organizing structure. However, whereas rock 'n' roll ignores the received conventions, 'progressive' pop inverts them, plays with them ironically, disrupts them, or produces shadows of them in new and unexpected forms. Frank Zappa purposefully breaks the rules and produces music which is frankly without tone (for instance, 'Uncle Meat'). Jimi Hendrix uses an untempered guitar. The Beatles use instrumentation to produce a kind of rhythm (violins in 'Eleanor Rigby', trumpets in 'Penny Lane'). Van Morrison uses repeated conventional cadences in an unusual way to provide the rhythmic foundation for 'Madame George' (on *Astral Weeks*). His unconventional use of this tradition is underlined in a highly self-conscious ironic emphasis at the end of the track when the classical bar structure and cadences disappear to be replaced by the 'pulse' repetition of 'goodbye, goodbye' which is slowly faded electronically in the manner of rock 'n' roll. In *Sergeant Pepper's Lonely Hearts Club Band* the Beatles experiment with simple chords and new progressions in a way which ignores the conventional rules.

The essential point in all this is that, unlike rock 'n' roll's, 'progressive' music's desertion of the conventional bar hierarchy, traditional harmonies and cadences did not also signify the disappearance of structure. 'Progressive' music had a commitment to larger forms, oppositions and variations, in a way which rock 'n' roll did not, and which is shown most clearly in the development of the 'concept album'. It exploited the break-up in convention accomplished by rock 'n' roll to combine both traditional and new elements in original and creative forms. At the same time, however, it maintained the essential original rock 'n' roll gain of timelessness and subversion of sequential form.

There was a partial move in 'progressive' music back towards melody – at least in relation to rock 'n' roll – but this was in no sense a reintroduction of the conventional bar structure or of classically prescribed cadences. The Beatles, in particular, were attracted to simple melodic chord singing but in an unconventional way. For instance, in 'Day In The Life' (the last track of the *Sergeant Pepper* LP) the conventional relation between the major dominant and the tonic is simply ignored in favour of the simple harmonies of the minor chords in E minor. Very typically for 'progressive' music the classic bar structure is disregarded and the music is allowed to float and vary. Again, we see the introduction of larger forms but not in a way which reproduces the older notion of exact temporal sequentiality.

If the foregoing is placed against the style, beliefs and consciousness of the hippies, we can see the basis for a striking homology and dialectical exchange of meanings, between a living culture and the internal forms of its music. The hippies were massively concerned with the attempt to subvert modern industrial time.[4] It was not for nothing that they threw away their watches during a trip, and generally refused to be accountable to 'normal' time. They were preoccupied with the 'now' and with the attempt to change or halt that flow of time which the bourgeois order had directed through a massive critical path of careful time calculations.

The hippies wanted to experience complexity and variation but of their own kind, in their own mode, and of their own making. They wanted to experience life not as a logic and rationality unfolding itself over time, but as an immediate richness occurring outside the dimension of time, or in another statement of the same thing, in the immediately apprehended 'now'. The ultimate in the experience of this complex varied richness was a glimpse of the mystic, divine state. A music which both attempted timelessness *and* an abstract, complex shape was marvellously formed both to mirror and momentarily complete this promethean attempt to encompass a post-capitalist timeless mysticism.

8 Conclusions:
Cultural politics

At its best ethnography does something which theory and commentary cannot: it presents human experience without minimizing it, and without making it a passive reflex of social structure and social conditions. It reproduces the profane creativity of living cultures. It breaks the spell of theoretical symmetry: drily proposed contradictions and problems become uncertainty, activity, effort, failure and success. Ethnography shows subjectivity as an active moment in its own form of production – not as a whispered bourgeois apology for a belief in individual sensibility.

i This book has aimed to bring out the material of two cultures and to show how oppressed or excluded social groups can creatively select, develop and transform aspects of their environment to make their own distinctive cultures.*i* These cultures do not follow the guide-lines of official culture, nor do they obey rules provided from outside or above. They are not even often recognized as unified cultures by agencies who pick up various fragmented aspects as 'social problems'. They have rejected or never received what is known, valued and revered. They live amid provided, cheap commodities: the shit of capitalist production. For all this, they have the essential, rare, irreverent gift of profanity: creativity.

This creativity is not free-floating. As we've seen, it evolves through its own form of material production and – through all the uncertainties, displacements and unintended consequences – it is applied to those real social locations and determinations which in the first place gave it birth. These cultures respond in a way which is more than random, they 'understand' in the logic of cultural action something of their own conditions of existence. Moreover, these complex responses are qualitatively different from unlocated theories outside themselves. The heroic, inescapable thing about these cultures is that their penetrations and insights are minutely involved with, and come from, a whole life-style, and concrete detailed transformations of particular cultural fields. Their massive, antagonistic, everyday, detailed pressure runs up against, seeks out, exposes, shows up innumerable facets, grains and weaknesses within the fine texture of the capitalist social system. It dramatizes, exploits, partially changes these things in material ways impossible for those *within* the grain of routine in everyday life. These cultures make their points – not through words – but through concrete transformation of objects, style, thought and consciousness. The dynamic transformation of their cultural field is the force of their argument. Their proofs are ways of living. We can learn from this cultural politics.

We have seen how both cultures took the unexplored side, the double edge, of commodities and cultural items around them to express and develop their own meanings. It is this achievement which the book is devoted to uncovering and exploring. In the course of this cultural development they were also, however, exploring some of the massive contradictions and tensions in modern society. Their located forms of creativity were taking what is radical and nascent in their parent cultures,[1] developing and delivering them in concrete ways – ways which themselves carry and live out great political significance. This was the distinctive form of what we can think of as their cultural politics.

In the very transformations of their cultural fields – no matter what was actually expressed – they were striking back at the heart of the whole commodity form and its detailed domination of everyday life. Instead of yielding control and allowing commodities – produced ever more centrally and ever more in a productive, not human, logic – to determine the pattern of commonplace life and modes of living, and behind this detail to enforce much larger ideological patterns, they seized a kind of control. No matter what the distorting, mediating links, they at least made some things in the world answerable to their own collective identity and *praxis*. These cultures reveal the unsuspected power of commodities and of a minutely articulated ideology in everyday life. They also show the room

171

and scope left by them and in them for struggle and change within the cells of everyday habit. We cannot now underestimate the importance of the struggle for an art in life, for change to be registered in the transformation of the small as well as in the large.

Their very use of everyday objects and transformation of unnoticed habits, then, made a larger and important political point. And though there was rarely any explicit political statement, they also made other innovatory and more direct criticisms of society. Although without a political voice cultural forms do speak through their very form, and movement and particular kind of production. The silent context of what makes certain practices meaningful, or gives them an internal logic and consistency, can be of profound political and critical importance. We must interrogate cultures, ask what are the missing questions they answer; probe the invisible grid of context; inquire what unsaid propositions are assumed in the visible and surprising external forms of cultural life. If we can supply the premises, dynamics, logical relations of responses which look quite untheoretical and lived out 'merely' as cultures, we will uncover a cultural politics – although, of course, disjointing what is most characteristic about it: its detailed incorporation and synthesis with a life-style and concrete forms of symbolic and artistic production.

Seen in this light, the hippy culture makes a penetrating criticism of the philistinism and inner contradictions of modern capitalist society. The hippies accepted a degree of decentredness and external determination of their own consciousness – common to us all but usually disguised – and explored it with the heroism of a full commitment of life-style. There was no barrier between thought and states of consciousness, between ideas and their implications for personal change. It was from the basis of organic individualism and spiritual intensity that the rest of society was viewed, and from which arose a potent critique of its rationalism, technicism and bureaucracy. It was against the touchstone of the uniqueness and richness of experience that they mocked conventional reality, and questioned always the meaning of development for development's sake, the inner-programmed rise of technology, the blind teleology of modern corporate organization, and the remoteness of modern institutions from human needs and uses. Their espousal of the rejected, hated and expelled inverted the conventional morality, questioned the whole notion of progress and suggested very different ways of valuing human qualities and achievements: failure could be success because it had avoided the ideologies which measured the difference.

The same perspective also produced a continuous and lived critique of the cultural bankruptcy of the organized left not only because the hippies remained unrecruited, but because the left ignored the whole cultural level and creative milieu in which the hippies were working, or wrote it off as simply deviant or irrelevant. They had no programme for the detailed and everyday.

Perhaps the sharpest penetration of the cultural politics of the hippies was their immanent critique of the protestant ethic,[2] and of its accelerating internal contradiction in late capitalism. The capitalist spirit has relied at least in part on self-denial, asceticism and devotion to duty to power its vast industrial achievements. In the late era of consumer capitalism, however, there is also a need for expanded consumption if expanded accumulation of capital and profit extraction is to continue. The primary sources for this consumer demand in the Western societies at least are no longer sufficient – even after Keynesian tuning of the market. More and more capitalism needs obvious, luxurious and unnecessary forms of consumption: it needs hedonism to maintain the driving-force of its asceticism. The protestant ethic needs its opposite in order to continue its own irrational progress. The hippies did not make this contradiction but they dramatized, exploited it – ground it out – in the minutiae of their life-style. They were the caricatured nightmarish incarnation of the bourgeoisie's own developing contradictory other nature. They did not earn, yet sublimely expected to survive. They watched and experienced nature as if there were no work to be done on it. They did not produce yet they consumed without guilt.

The strange *cerebral* hedonism with which these things were acted out – the acceptance of damnation, the celebration of the present, the negation of the iron hope of the future – all unpicked the logic of puritan conviction from within as well as mocking it from without. It played across the strict anachronism of a modern cultural puritanism. As the potential is increasing for individuals to express themselves and break through repressive internal and external controls and lift somewhat the weight of the 'reality principle', their ability to do so is decreasing. The hippies mark a kind of eruption of the cultural id through the restrictive super-ego of social convention. They provide an exaggerated, lopsided, caricatured burlesque show of what reality could be for the majority.

In a related way the hippies subverted and disorganized received notions of time. Industrial society relies upon a careful, consistent and sequential ordering of time. It is the dependable measurement and control of time which is the spine of capitalist organization: it is the means by which it knows what it is doing, and the medium in which it extracts surplus value. To insist on the relativity of time, on its relation to subjective states, on its infinite philosophic variability, on its irrelevance to natural, cyclic or industrial routine, is to bewilder rationalist organization and the capitalist calculation of profit. The rejection of work by the hippies was in part a rejection of the whole time-frame which made it meaningful and regulated its moving parts. It may be expected that more struggles and tensions of the future will take experiential forms of challenge to rationalist, ordered notions of time.

The motor-bike boys, too, working on their own received class experiences, and perceiving society from a different class location, *lived out* important criticisms and insights. The premises which make their culture meaningful, and against which their actions can be seen to be neither random nor arbitrary, make important proto-political points. Their reorganization of sets of meanings, their unusual adaptations of the signifiers and rituals of conventional institutions, such as the media and the church, the concrete formation of a human life-style through the materials of technology, also show elements not only of insights into, but of a creative response to, modern conditions. They show one form of lying down with the lion.

The modern urban and technical environment is a source of fear, uncertainty and alienation for many. Their surroundings seem to be forces over people rather than their obedient creations. Capitalism needs and has created gigantic technologies for its own advance, but is at the same time terrified of them, of the dehumanization they bring. The bikeboys' adaption and taming of a fierce technology for a symbolic human purpose highlights this contradiction and shows us just how far the rest of conventional society is from controlling the Frankenstein it has created. The mastery of the alienation of the machine, its answerability to the most minute experiential forms of the bike culture, dramatize the widening gap elsewhere between more inturned and nervous sensibilities and the gargantuan, cyclopean forces which are their creation. The capitalist, industrial apotheosis will be the final destruction of human scale. Its most extraordinary achievements will be impossible to live in. The robustness of the bike culture shows us the fragility of urban sensibility, and the humanized motor-bike shows us the terror of gigantic technologies.

The directness and irreverence of the motor-bike boys is also a challenge to institutional forms of politeness. Their spontaneity and lack of formality in social relations highlight the restrictions of a bureaucratic, neighbour-watching conformism. The roar of the motor-bike, or the menace of physical, masculine presence show how the learned lines of demarcation are social products, and, despite their restriction and enforced sacrifice of expression and autonomy, are no protection against the sword of those who do not respect their values. The piratical, outrageous air of the bikeboys lives off, finds its meaning and clumsy grace from the ludicrous orderedness of the rest of us. They show just how easy it is to be a pirate when the rest of us wear grey. Our incorporated, bureaucratic, mindless existence is the air through which the motor-bike exhaust tears and crackles.

To the definite cultural achievements of the hippies and bikeboys must be added therefore, in their different ways, real critical achievements – at least at the level of a cultural politics. Despite this, however, it is precisely in the larger arena of politics proper that these cultures met their final, tragic limits – limits which raise the whole question of the status and viability of cultural politics and of a struggle waged exclusively at the level of life-style.

The very density and intensity of the bike and hippy cultures, the way in which they turned upon response and detailed transformations, drove out any long-term analysis of their situation. The cultures never worked back single-mindedly to the causes of the suffering, oppression and exclusion of their members. Though profoundly organized and sensitized by class, and though working on the sub-text of the dominant reification of the commonplace and commonsense, their responses contained no class analysis of fundamental causes and therefore no real chance of changing the world. Quite apart from the wider political implications, and evaluations of such change, the point remains a formal one. It would have been the only way to secure the conditions for their own long-term survival. The silent contexts and premises needed to be spoken and pushed through into larger forms of cultural and political action if their really determining circumstances were to be modified. Their oppositional and radical themes were worked out instead in immediate materials and along seams of meaning which did not challenge the basic structures and institutions of society.

If their cultures were basically a matter of style, then no matter what they expressed or implied they could be taken as just that: style which could be generalized, torn from its precise contextual meaning, and used to generate further demand for the culture and consciousness consumer industries. The dazzling world of changes they made in their immediate lives and in their own proper cultural fields left unchallenged the larger world of political and social institutions which were the material base for the experience of the classes from which they came. Though stupendously outmanoeuvred and embarrassed at a day to day level, the dominant class remained supreme in its control of the most basic cultural patterns of life for the majority. No matter what larger world these cultures renewed in their imaginations, they reproduced the real world here by default or lack of interest.

The detailed, informal and lived can enjoy its victory in a larger failure. The reproduction of more complex forms of social organization may even take the form of ideological inversions and experimentations in local cultural politics. If it is to even maintain its own existence, never mind its subversion into complex forms of its opposite, the detailed dialectics of cultural transformation and personal liberation must also stretch to a dialectic with political and material structures.

In one sense the achievements of the bikeboys and the hippies were profoundly premature: post-revolutionary cultural responses to pre-revolutionary social, political and organizational problems. The working out of contradictions at a creative, cultural level played back a remarkable light on the larger contradictions of society, but could not resolve or work them through because they arose at a different and more basic plane. Their resolution would have to be made at their own level. Though real and concrete and involving their own forms of production, the responses and innovations of the bikeboys and hippies were nevertheless most basically cultural sublimations of fundamental contradictions. The cultures penetrated, exposed and partially and locally resolved these contradictions, but only in a special disconnected and informal way which left their basic structures unaltered. It is almost that the cultures, in their silent contexts, lived as if the basic structures *were* changed – enjoying that in imagination while making no attempt to bring it about in reality. It is this prolepsis which is often the motor for a cultural politics – and also its final tragic limit.

In the case of the motor-bike boys, for instance, although they had mastered a technology in their leisure and pioneered embryonic forms – or developed and made explicit working-class themes – of living with technology, they made no attempt to apply these insights to their working situation. They did not make demands, or pioneer changes there for more humanized systems of work – or even see any connections between technology in their leisure and the most massive application of technology of all: machinery in work. Not only this, but they uncritically accepted the current organization of production and their lowly place within it as well as the legitimacy of a whole range of other institutions – though making, of course, their own local and creative adaptations – which maintain and reproduce society in its present form, and which ultimately outlawed or displaced their own culture.

There were further aspects of a larger political failing. If the bikeboys took strands from their parent class culture and creatively developed them, they also unconsciously took and reproduced, often in more virulent forms, less progressive

177

aspects of working-class culture. Their racism, for instance, was quite marked, and the concrete secure life-style from which it sprang was actually predicated on a naturalized exclusion of politics and of larger concepts of whole classes sharing similar material circumstances and acting on this basis. Although they had mastered a form of technology, they had not mastered their social relations with one another and with other members of their class. The fighting, violence and outrage which was mainly a symbolic presence polarized the bikeboys from other working-class groups. It could break out and cause injury to others, and, sometimes, finally to the self as in the motor-bike death. The forces of life spoke strangely through death in the culture. This ambience tragically sealed the bike culture off and abnegated any role it might have had in the larger development of the working class, and the struggle for change in those conditions and contradictions to which, if not in words, its own presence spoke.

In some respects, the hippies' culture posed more trenchant criticisms of conventional society. It also partly replaced or rejected some of its main institutions. This may well explain the relatively longer life and influence of the hippy as compared with that of the bike culture. If we take the pivotal area of work and attitude to the production process, for instance, we find that the hippies did indeed reject existing attitudes and practices: they did not work. But even here there was no attack on the basis of work, or struggle with its definitions from the inside. The culture privately maintained its own rhythms and sense of time which constituted a profound exposure and criticism of industrial time, but it did not take them out to challenge the time-sheet and ordered time in their generating heartlands: the factories and bureaucracies. Their critical perspective was purchased at the price of withdrawal and their insight was reserved for the cognoscenti. Their culture was actually predicated on a degree of exclusion. This circumscription of their sphere of influence left the culture itself on a shrinking isthmus with no plan for changing the tides, except in its own imagination, which was to engulf it.

We can see at the heart of the hippy culture precisely this imaginative but impotent grappling with gigantic forces. They broke open some of the profound processes producing our late urban capitalism. They saw into the balance of freedom and determination, into the fragile construction of human subjectivity in relation to material determinations and the play of ideology masking itself as naturalism. But instead of turning the force of this insight on to the external world and struggling for its change, they turned the force back in on themselves and on the minute transfixing, undiscovered contours of their own natures. They discovered a world there, but it was a trapped world. Citizenship there disenfranchised them from the real world – often with tragic personal results. The all-time gap the hippies proclaimed between the hip and the straight ruled out strategies for passage from one to the other, ruled out dialectical notions of the relationship between them, ruled out plans for breaking down or progressively reconstituting that divide. The dialectics of the world spun too closely in the exotic centre of their own spirituality. There was a betrayal, finally, of the principle of human agency.

It was precisely this spiritual intensity – not a progressive radicalism – which supplied the basis for their criticism of society. They were humanist/religious criticisms of rationalism, technicism and bureaucracy – not of capitalism as such. At the worst this was a dark romantic rejection of modernism pure and simple: a moody negation which did not work through, sum up, save and take to a higher level the best that exists – the proper transcending of a social system and stage of development – but resisted everything in mystical enigma.

In one way we can see the whole espousal by the hippies of the rejected, hated and expelled – the lumpen – as a vehicle and symbol and celebration of this. It is interesting that their lived metaphors were not drawn from progressive social elements, and were not then exploited for their political content. The lumpen was not turned to as a social base for change, revolt or achievement of a non-utopian socialism, but as a superstitious retreat from what existed, as a material protection and milieu for the journeys of the mind. In this they were finally, characteristically, representative of the long, one-sided romance between bohemia and the lumpenproletariat. This identification sums up both the strengths and weaknesses of the hippies. They were allied with the poor and rejected, lived out a sympathy with their spirit, heroically and creatively took it further, but did not organize to change it: ultimately they were comforted, not outraged, by it.

In this charting of limitations we must not be too simplistic, nor goad ourselves into builders of better realities than reality can manage. We cannot enter a cultural supermarket, choose this and that, pass other things by, take what is good, leave the rest and pay the variable bill at a check-out to the future. Many weaknesses are the connected obverse of strength. Many strengths grow only in the protection of weakness and withdrawal. Human productions are all of a piece, indivisible and always summed. The metal cannot be simply smelted out from the ore of experience in human affairs.

Our whole case here really bears on the nature of cultural politics, not on any catalogue of detailed failings in the hippy or bike cultures. Every limit we mark is riveted to a peculiar strength. We cannot hail the one and condemn the other without recognizing their specific, particular, concrete forms of combination. Nor should we think that any particular category or definition can be, or could have been, easily rectified while keeping unchanged other things which are valued. Furthermore it is mean-spirited, uncharitable and pedantic to list all the things these cultures were not, when they so clearly were *something* – something where little or nothing had been before and which teaches us about a whole unexpected range of cultural struggle and transformation. The whole point about these cultures is that they show by example how larger solutions, political programmes and theoretical perspectives utterly fail to supply or even sense the importance of the cultural level, of transformation in detail, of change in routine and daily consciousness. It is this achievement which must be preserved – those asses on those lines – and not the wool of armchair-might-have-beens. To have had the cultures any other way – as the criticisms might imply is possible – would have been to destroy them, or to have made them into something else altogether. Life is the arbiter of conjunction in forms – not our conceits.

With these two cultures, then, the balance-sheet of success and failure cannot be duly filled, one half torn away, condemned to the past, and one half inflated into a future. The connection is more intrinsic than that. In the ethnography we saw many of the detailed connections, but I would like to end with a more speculative notion of the connection between the detailed cultural forms and their larger failings. This is that the levels were articulated by a formation of compulsion and tragedy.

It might be suggested that it was partly the intensity and isolation caused by the larger political failings which generated the particular mystique and power of transformation in the cultural fields of these groups. They were a crucially modern urban phenomenon in exemplifying the tragic tension which can be generated when individuals and groups wage an undirected but unremitting, unequal struggle against the unrecognized, unknown or misunderstood, determining social and economic structures around them. The central failure of this promethean struggle in the bike and hippy cultures provided a thousand axes for life-styles to spin back into themselves. And in this spinning, small transformations, heroic confrontations and real forms of cultural production were made which broke open the whole undiscovered potential of daily life. If the exploitation of trivial commodities, and of the manipulation of routine: of an art in life.

Once the cultures are in train, they must be lived through, the road taken, the conviction carried on, and this very movement commits you to finding a solution there is no way of achieving – without action at an altogether different and more collective level: that level which is already denied in the logic of the culture. Ultimately the force must be turned inwards to maintain the pitch of the drama. The power of finality and solution is turned back on to forms of desperate personal transformation and even destruction of the self: not experienced by all, but known to all, and at the symbolic centres of the cultures as in the bike or drug death. Personal intensity, suffering and destruction is a destination of kinds when others recede. It marks an opting out of the heave of historical time into a final sublimation of an impossible project. But this fatal flaw also provides the energy and eyes of the gods. It motors a creativity and vitality which is far from fatalism and pessimism. We may speculate that it was this basic centripetal force which gave the bike and hippy cultures in different ways their mystique, power and revelatory qualities: the pinpoint of burning creative pressure which dragged through a cultural politics after them. Their profane acid scaled off the pretences and illusions of the bourgeois order and allowed new production in their own cultural fields to penetrate through and show the possibility of the revolutionary in the small, detailed and everyday.

This widened range of human involvement and activity is irreversible and must now be included in grander schemes for change. Theory must learn from life. A genuine politics must come up from the people, from cultural politics, as well as down from theory, or the political party. This is especially important to remember as the political and economic crises of the 1970s seem to pre-empt all other issues. We can learn this from the cultures presented in this book – but not in a false and easy fraternity. Their elevation was bought at a price. The work remains to develop a cultural politics not based on isolation and despair.

Epilogue

At various stages and after numerous drafts, I tried to contact members of the bike and hippy cultures I had known and taped conversations with during my field work. I have still not been able to get in touch with any of the bikeboys, to show them this book, but I have, however, been in contact with some of the hippies several times. One of them agreed to formulate some responses to the book:

Prologue   December 1976

TJ   Died in Morocco. Circumstances not verifiable. Rumoured that the cause was a dirty works. Medical assistance not available.

JIN   Terminal cancer of the liver. Became one of the first of the few experimental subjects. His reward was 42 pills of heroin and 36 pills of cocaine. He was the most informed person I ever met.

A and S These two were brothers and made a suicide-pact. Each ate half a bottle of tuinal. After sleeping for three days A woke up to find S had electrocuted himself by falling on the bedside lamp. I was an unofficial witness. A fell off Clifton Suspension Bridge one week later because the gas oven had made him sick.

G   He had been a close friend at one time but he took far too much acid. He rested his

183

	head on a railway line and let BR do it for him.
M	Did a burglary after eating too many MX. When the police came he went on to the roof, stumbled and hit the pavement head first. He looked like a sack full of red ink.
PJ	He OD'd four times on barks and four times the medics saved him. On the fifth occasion the crew took his pulse and sat on the end of the bed smoking a cigarette each before they carried him out dead. Each of us dropped a red carnation on his coffin before they shovelled in the earth.
A Z	A sensitive and gentle guy. If he could not get junk he would jack up aspirin, he even jacked up in the fingers which had once made music.
S D	He once told me that he had murdered his stepfather and run away. He showed me five passports all under different nationalities. He acquired his sixth and is no more.
R	I still feel angry when I think of what they did to him. He had no secrets from anyone. He kept a diary open on his table for anyone to read. The law caught him and sent him to prison where he became ill. He was sent to hospital but the authorities hijacked him back to prison, where he died. Post-mortem held in secret.

Preamble

What you have just read are the deletions from the list. They are the terminations, names and cyphers that have been erased from the list. The dog-eared, grey folder which contains the list exists somewhere in a dusty, dull, drab, air-conditioned office.

To the clerk who makes the additions and subtractions it is another typing chore of some 2,000 names. We, the names on that list, are nobodies, ghosts, are waiting. We know we have three choices. We can stay on it to be watched, observed, analysed, sanctioned. We can move to erasure, termination, have a coroner's report and death cert. attached. We will still exist on the list as a statistic. Or third, we can become inactive. When the control agencies have no information of our activities to add, it can be assumed that we have left the area or are pursuing worthwhile social existences, but what I may add is their value-judgment. I often ask myself in private moments: Did they want to go, or were they pushed? Perhaps they chose the pursuit of nirvana as a career, and in a brief moment of despair, had decided to 'clock out'. Some with a loud clang, not even bothering to look over their shoulder and others no doubt timidly pressing down on the time handle, waiting, listening for it to trip. Leaving only the faintest pink skeletal mark upon the buff.

Perhaps you consider it idle speculation to pursue this line of thought, thinking these people were not in your bag. I would reply to you that they were in someone's bag. They were in my bag, for a start. They impinged on my life. If you look at the list, you will see my name, and we on the list are well beyond your pale. Consider yourselves fortunate indeed.

We the brother and sisterhood of the grey folder are monitored by the control agencies, our only chance of freedom is to escape to other countries where the control agencies do not exist but in doing so we become disenfranchised. Or perhaps get lost in another locality where we may be overlooked for a time. We exist as snowmen. Obstinate and oblivious to the heat of the political sun, waiting for the next ice age. It will never come.

Epilogue

It will soon be Christmas, and I can't face it! It's a depressing and hollow ritual – I went to town yesterday with a quarter bottle of vodka inside me. At one point the noisy crowd became insufferable, so I stood in a doorway and jammed my fingers in both ears. Looking across the street, the last-minute shoppers drifted by like ghostly ants, anxious haunted expressions on their faces as they stumbled through the blue light towards the

New Year. I had seen those expressions before in newspaper pictures taken in Vietnam, and more recently, Soweto.

And you ask for a couple of thousand Lego images that if correctly assembled may induce tomorrow's self-seekers to disregard all signposts. What's the word from Johannesburg? Here it is, Happy Christmas, everybody's having fun, look to the future, it's only just begun. More repeats!

What about the past seven years? Horrific, Happy, Depressingly Beautiful, Paranoid years. Those were the days when in a benign pre-lysergic cocoon I would be distracted by the television, but not any more. Being a dummy is hard work! My crazed stupidity impels me towards the same carrot that your publishers have dangled in front of you. Bite their hands and eat the carrot, it will improve your vision. Do your own publishing. The Sycophants from the Home Counties are dying the death, why prolong their misery. Nirvana is not a five-hundred-quid front cover illustration. It will not shield you from their plague.

Reading your book is difficult for me, because I cannot assimilate all your technical phrases. It does, however, jog my memory. I suppose I was no less naïve then than I am now. That's a thought I find frightening. What I have learnt in the past seven years is how to lose myself! I can disappear in a crowd. I know how to homogenize but so have the control agencies. I continuously develop my ability to discriminate between all groups and I find myself belonging to none.

Discriminating,

Disassociated,

Disenfranchised,

And I am no nearer to getting at the truth.

I think that the problem we are now confronted with is what is the best way to keep open the old frontiers. It is important that ordinary people be allowed to travel overseas as much as possible, particularly young people, for it is they who can adjust most readily to other cultural values. To evaluate what is good and reject things that are unnecessary is the only way to survive. Travellers will also gain insight into the nature of propaganda, particularly the narrow nationalistic variety. Someday someone is going to invent an aerosol spray that will change the colour of our skin. When that day comes, the international itinerant will be King. We will have become a band of gypsies absorbing anything useful, be it sustenance for our bodies or minds.

Perhaps losing all my battles, I can win some kind of war, but gazing at the enemy ranks, shielded and unmoved by my rantings, I lose all hope. The masonic infantry including judges, high-ranking police officers, politicians, businessmen, etc. Or perhaps the media cavalry armed with books, video tape and newspaper drowning me in a morass of propaganda. The only truths to be found are elsewhere overseas. I used to dream that when I accumulated enough money this is where I will go. Somewhere else in order that I may discharge my responsibilities without envious moralizing sanction.

Such is the progress of a pilgrim, the new frontiers are not of this planet.

First addition, February 1977

SP: There were two South Americans from Brazil on a bus. Sat behind them were two policemen, off duty. The one Brazilian was telling the other about where he was going to score some dope. When they got off the bus, the police followed at a discreet distance.

                     They arrived outside the house and were jumped on by the law.

                     Reinforcements came and the Brazilians were then made to ring the door-bell.

                     When the door opened, uniforms swarmed everywhere.

                     The occupants of the house were a guy and his wife and a small baby girl.

                     All three were taken to the station, the adults being required to make statements.

                     The Brazilians were asked for statements which they readily provided. They were charged with conspiracy to buy cannabis and were fined £25 each for doing so.

The occupants of the house were charged jointly with possession and supplying cannabis. A week after being charged the guy had a mental breakdown and was admitted to a mental hospital where I went to see him. He had previously regarded me as a good friend, but when he saw me walk through the doors of the ward he ran away. During the next eight weeks, I took him to the magistrates' courts, first, for him to be remanded awaiting medical reports, and finally, to be tried alongside his wife. They were fined something like £200 between them. When they were in dock together, they did not speak to each other, or for that matter their eyes did not even meet.

The guy is still attending the mental hospital as an out-patient. Their marriage has broken down and the child who once had a father now only has a devoted mother to rely on.

This happened four years ago!

One of the policemen volunteered for duty in Belfast. The other policeman joined the drug squad and he and the guy he first busted are on the best of terms.

They drink together.

But he is still on the list.

Theoretical appendix

Socio-symbolic homologies: a theory of cultural forms

This appendix sets out formally the theoretical view of cultural development and genesis informing the presentation of the main text. It provides some technical terms and distinctions which might aid those concerned with rigorous model-building or with their own social research.

The following is both a theory of located cultural forms and a suggested method of approach to, and analysis of, concrete cultures. The two are always linked – whether it is made explicit or not.

I take the essence of located cultural forms to be their constitutive relationships: the way the social group is connected to the objects, artefacts, institutions and systematic practices of others which surround it. Such relationships need *not* imply conscious purpose or intention on the part of the social group – though this may play a role even if it does bring unexpected outcomes. Changed consciousness is certainly a result of certain kinds of relationship. This view of cultural relation *does* imply real exchanges and material dialectics between the structure of human subjectivity, its characteristic sensibilities, and its contexts.

Some relations, of course, are not reciprocal or centred within the group. The commercial system, productive relations, ideological and political formations intervene, pervert, redirect or block the possibility of intent, pure expression or absolute harmony. This does not, however, deconstruct the cultural level or transfer completely away from it the production and generation of its own meanings. There are reciprocal relations even through these mediations, external constraints and

189

intrusion of wider meanings. The effort of cultural analysis in any specified region is precisely to gauge their number and importance, locate them and chart their internal processes and final influence.

I suggest that cultural relationships in any specified culture – and they can be taken at successive levels of generality – should be analysed in three modes:

(1) the indexical;
(2) the homological;
(3) the integral.

1 The indexical

For the purposes of our analysis the indexical concerns the degree to which external items are related to a social group in a general quantitative sense, i.e. for how long a group listens to pop music, where and how often. The analysis is indexical precisely because the interest is in assessing how outside items are 'indexed' to a social group. We may call the sum of these the 'indexical field'.

The indexical field of most of us would include, for instance, houses and cars, pop music, *Coronation Street*, commodities of all kinds and natural landscapes. For our purposes the variation of the indexical level is quantitative. It can record differences in duration and frequency of contact but it cannot explain the significance of this variation in a meaningful way. It may simply be random or arbitrary from the point of view of the social group.

Of course, this does not mean that indexical relations are without importance. On the contrary, it is through the medium of such relationships that the tyranny of the commodity form is enforced, and through which the slow drip of conventional daily habit, supported by institutions, state agencies and the systematic practices of others, wears in to subjectivity the shape of larger ideologies. There is undoubtedly a one-way determination of meaning of the profoundest importance. This is the realm of ideology. It is one of the most basic constitutive categories of the human sciences.

The theory outlined here, however, is not oriented to pick up these importances. It can be seen as a qualification of larger theories of ideology as they bear in upon the level of located cultures and subjectivity. It investigates the degree to which the collective activity of human groups can roll back somewhat the one-way determination of their own meanings and sensibilities. It accepts the possibility that there may be a reciprocal determining influence between a human group and what surrounds it: that indexical fields may contain smaller and, as it were, differently polarized fields which are *not* random with respect to particular social groups.

2 The homological

This level concerns the differentiation of the relationships which the indexical stage of the analysis has identified for us. Essentially it is concerned with how far, in their structure and content, particular items parallel and reflect the structure, style, typical concerns, attitudes and feelings of the social group. Where homologies are found they are actually best understood in terms of structure. It is the continuous play between the group and a particular item which produces specific styles, meanings, contents and forms of consciousness. The artefact, object or institution in such a relationship must consistently serve the group at a number of levels with meanings, particular attitudes, bearings and certainties. It must help to support, return and substantiate particular kinds of social identity and the practice and application of particular kinds of sensibility – conscious and unconscious, voluntary and automatic. Items which have this kind of relationship to a social group are likely to be differentially sought out and pursued by, rather than be simply randomly proximate to, a social group. We may say that all such items constitute the 'cultural field' of a social group. The cultural field is always smaller than the indexical field.

Homological analysis of a cultural relation is synchronic. It is not equipped to account for changes over time, or to account for the creation or disintegration, of homologies: it records the complex qualitative state of a cultural relationship as it is observed in one quantum of time.

We are all related to several artefacts and objects at an homological level, but it is likely that we will only be significantly related to a few of them. Relationships are likely to be more carefully articulated and selectively pursued with expressive artefacts but they may perfectly well arise with functional objects, institutions or the natural environment.

Homological analysis is considerably more interpretative than indexical analysis. It is not possible to present it simply in the terms of the actors themselves. Their explicit consciousness is more a variable result of, rather than a determinant or read-out display of cultural process. Indeed there will often be contradictions between verbal statements by the actors, and their behaviour, interaction and between these and symbolic meanings carried in the various cultural forms of bodily style and expression as well as in the characteristic use and development of items in their cultural field. There are two distinctive moments in homological analysis: the examination of the social group; the examination of their preferred cultural items.

There are, of course, real difficulties in determining the structure and form, of the sensibility, values and attitudes of particular social groups – not least because these things are never expressed directly but in media and through cultural items in a way which, I argue, helps to constitute the social group in the first place, and which are themselves likely to be objects of study in the second stage of the analysis. An unremittingly qualitative, or ethnographic method is called for to establish the greatest possible number of valid channels for the examination of the social group, and levels of its expression and development, and in particular to give direct access to its language and behaviour over time. In this way the main structures of feeling and attitude in the social group can be 'triangulated' back from its various expressions, actions and cultural formations. It is in this complex, multi-based, grounding of the analysis that the distorting effect of particular media can be minimized and a defence in depth set up against a tautologous overdetermination of the whole analysis by particularly strong items of the social group's cultural field.

There are difficulties of a different sort in the second stage of the analysis. It is clear that different groups can be involved with the same cultural items and yet take different homological meanings and effects from them. It is also clear that what a particular group makes of a particular item can change over time, so that what was once accepted is rejected. A particular item is not, then, changeless, absolute and specific in its cultural meaning. It is not as if a fully constituted 'content' always draws forth a predictable response. Objects, artefacts and institutions do not, as it were, have a single valency. It is the act of social engagement with a cultural item which activates and brings out particular meanings. On the other hand, there is not a limitless scope for the production of meanings. I argue for a more structural analysis of the 'objective possibilities' of particular items in an assessment of their role in cultural relationships.

A *Participant observation*[1]

Before discussing the technique and theory of Participant Observation, it is necessary to specify the object of the method and in particular the status and generality of the human experience it seeks to explore and expose. I do not see society as a series of disconnected individuals living out their own particular lives, but as a structured whole within which individuals and groups live under differing degrees of domination, expressing *and reproducing* in different degrees through symbolic patterns and cultural practices a sense of *positionality* within and perhaps resistance to the hidden, misunderstood or unseen overarching structures which limit their field of choices and help to constitute them in the first place.

My interest in human experience, therefore, is not focused on separated, individuated, idiosyncratic, subjectivity and consciousness, but on the subjective dimension of what is *shared;* of the symbolic, organizational structure along which particular subjectivities lie – the most immediate frame which helps to produce, and is partly produced by, subjectivity, and which is the first great articulation of the individual and society and organized expression of opposition and identity. What is shared, maintained, reproduced and generated by the social group, as distinct from the free-floating individual consciousness, is the crucial focus in my notion of subjectivity.

The group is the smallest unit of cultural existence. It is the smallest unit of resistance against the dominant culture, and the immediate form of protection of, and influence on, *particular* subjectivities. It is the pivotal site for the development of wider social and cultural practices. Though the *material* of experience is necessarily often collected (as a research act) from the individual, and though the expression and form of this experience may be personal, the real generator of this experience is the interaction of the group within a specific social and material matrix of symbols, expectations and conditions. Though subjective, then, the focus of my interest is on the *subjectivity* of symbolic systems, actions and values, *not* on the individual person; or more correctly it is only on the individual as he lives out personalized versions of collective strategies.

In the preconceptions of the observer, in the artificiality of the observer/observed situation, in the decentration, partiality, inversion or distortion of self-knowledge in the observed, lie many possible sources of error in the participant observation method. Furthermore, replication and proof are impossible and a scientistic concern with technique can never conceal – only impinge and obstruct – the proper working through of participant observation in its own forms of production and work on human meaning. For the difficulties and peculiar characteristics of participant observation constitute finally a distinctive problematic: a particular kind of complex relationship which determines its own practices. I argue for three, basic linked strategies in the method:

(i) That the scope of distortion inherent in the participant observation problematic should be minimized as far as is reasonably possible by 'holding to the natural'.

(ii) That a range of methods should be used to 'cross-grid' the evidence and so further reduce distortion.

(iii) That finally the specific and finally irreducible problematic of the Participant Observation method should be used as a resource in a 'self-reflexive' analysis – not regarded as the implicit limits of 'scientific inquiry'.

i Holding to the natural – the naturalistic technique

Participant observation has certain intrinsic advantages over other methods of inquiry. The most important of these is that the research is done in the natural situation of the actors. This intrinsic advantage can be strengthened.

The researcher should be as flexible as possible, and suspend so far as possible specific theories – while admitting his general theoretical orientation – for the explanation of what he expects to encounter. He should spend time acclimatizing himself to particular situations before making efforts to collect material of any kind. He should try to avoid the initiation of activities in the group. During group discussions, for instance, although the researcher may start with general questions he should aim to generate a 'take off' whereby the discussion goes into areas quite unsolicited by him.

Group discussions provide not only an important source of data, but a control on the reliability of the data and a guarantee of a kind of validity – especially in view of the proposed unit of focus of the whole method: the social group. An individual by himself can mislead the researcher because there is no *other* immediate source of counter-evidence. Unless there is a group-wide conspiracy against the researcher, however, the mutual historical knowledge of constituent group members usually prevents any particular individual 'telling the story' and encourages individuals to express more what is common to all.

Furthermore, the participant observer's exogenous determination of particular social situations is likely to be lessened where the researcher is in the natural surroundings, and in the presence of a group: the endogenous determinants are likely to swamp the marginal effect of the observer's presence. There are also enormous advantages of data retrieval in recording group discussions. The disruption caused by the tape-recorder is likely to be minimal in the group situation, and where several discussions are conducted over time, insignificant.

ii   Cross-gridding of evidence – the comparative technique

Another important way in which the scope of 'bias' can be diminished is to gather data in a number of ways, and in different situations, and to note contradictions between different sorts of data. It may be, for instance, that data collected during an informal interview may contradict or question data, say, arising from a group discussion, or data collected by the researcher directly through observation. Language is a code and *not* a direct representation of reality. There are many other codes of signification. The researcher needs to be open to all the kinds of communication used in a particular cultural setting, and to all the implicit contradictions between the different codes and between the substantive meanings communicated in the different codes. These contradictions need to be recognized, contextualized and, if possible, explained. As a particular pattern emerges from one set of data, evidence collected by different methods may 'autonomously' contradict the developing thesis and point to ways in which the data have been wrongly taken, skewed or wrongly interpreted. Partly the evidence may be given scope to act in this way by the theoretical openness of the researcher at the beginning of his field work. Partly 'autonomy' can be encouraged by the use of a number of methods so that the evidence relating to the same area can be cross-gridded, or, in Cicourel's term 'triangulated', and divergences noted.

In one sense this is a deconstruction of the 'participant observation' method into its related and constitutive elements. Particular mixes of these techniques can be used according to the nature of the research task. I list below the cluster of methods I drew on in this research:

Participant Observation
Observation
Just Being Around
Group Discussions
Recorded Discussions
Informal Interview
Use of Existing Surveys.

iii The self-reflexive technique and analytic moment

So far we have looked at how the scope of 'distortion' in the participant observation problematic can be limited. This is an argument, borrowing from the naturalist, classic perspective, for damping down the 'flux' in 'communication systems', for limiting 'bias' in the data. However, whereas in the classical method this is done in the name of objectivity so that remaining 'problems' are seen as the source of unfortunate residual distortion, I argue for the use of the naturalistic comparative techniques to specify more precisely what is the *scope* and *meaning* of the essential problematic of the method. Instead of being 'problems', the final and 'unresolvable' difficulties of the method are its specific resources. These moments concern the ability of the researcher to reflexively analyse the intersection of his own social paradigms with those of the people he wishes to understand. Such an intersection speaks, of course, as much to the researcher and his world as it does of any other world.

There are times at which the researcher feels threatened; there are times when he knows he cannot follow; there are times when the role 'researcher' becomes inadequate, empty, even dishonest; there are times when he is asked to declare his 'real' self; there are times when his own 'commonsense' faces another very different and disorienting 'commonsense'; there are times when he feels he should step out of his relatively passive role and act to help, save or denounce. It is precisely these things which are conventionally bracketed as dangerous and damaging: they are subsumed under 'going native', 'loss of perspective' or 'emotional reaction', 'unscientific response'. Usually thought of as unavoidable costs, the 'problems' of field work can be more imaginatively thought of as the result of a fine intersection of two subjective meaning constructions. The points of contact and conflict have profound significance for the understanding of fundamental differences between social worlds, between characteristic and routinized structures of feeling, consciousness and thought. This is the real validity of the method: the collision of meanings and subjective constructions at *commensurate* levels. These destructive moments provide the mapping points for another's reality. It is in this complex process that we can speak of 'empathy'. Although the researcher can never experience another experience – the romantic notion of 'empathy' – he can feel how his own experience is minutely locked into another's: how his own experience is contradicted or disoriented. The 'problems' of this method always ask questions. If the researcher feels threatened at certain points, what is it that threatens him? If the researcher does not feel able to join in certain group activities, what is stopping him? If the researcher feels that the group is trying to strip away his role of researcher what does this imply? Answers to these questions begin the construction of overlapping worlds. The researcher can 'read' the moments of his own distress to map the dark sides of others' worlds.

This is not to suggest that one achieves 'knowledge' or hard data from the self-reflexive technique, or that the moments of internal disorientation are of intrinsic value or should be passed on to others. It is to suggest that the germs of insight are born here which can then be tested against evidence collected in other ways. If such insight is conceived not from the complex tension and stress arising from a social relationship, but out of blindness or illusion, then the 'autonomous' power of the evidence will discredit it. On the other hand, if 'hunches' are borne out by reliable naturalistic data and cross-grids of other evidence collected in different ways and at different times, and if they progressively explain or enlighten contradictions in the data, then a more substantial understanding can be developed. Such 'hunches' will quickly gather corroborative material around them, and can ultimately be presented more 'object-ively' without the uncertainty of the original germination.

B The 'objective possibilities' of cultural items

Broadly there seem to be three possibilities in the analysis of a cultural item. It could be argued that its value and meaning is totally socially given. That is: the item itself is a cypher, without inherent structure or meaning, so that it is the social group and its expectations which supply a content. There is extreme difficulty, of course, in explaining why it should be one item and not another, one whole *genre* and not another, which is taken as the receptacle for particular kinds of socially created meanings and values. One could only explain this most basically in terms of historical accident. It could be, for instance, that a certain group is naturally exposed to certain music, so that proximity breeds a relationship which is, in the beginning, accidental in the sense that there is nothing intrinsic in the art-form which makes it, and no other form, suitable for a certain group. Once this original point of contact is made, then the process might become more continuous and directional.

Because the original group value the art-form, later groups take over what they imagine to be established ways of appreciating it. Accumulation and substantiation through time could develop into what looks like a fully-blown 'aesthetic' so that people assume values and meanings to be located within the art-form rather than in their perceptions of it. Other art-forms may be rejected on the apparent basis of their intrinsic inferiority. Values held to be within the art-form may be defended as having a substantial and autonomous existence. In fact, those values, and those imagined superiorities, would be nothing more than the accumulated, located reflections of a particular way of life 'read' into the music. In this sense, a cultural item is like a mirror linked to a memory bank, holding, but without an intrinsic or transformative grasp, valued and significant images derived in the first place from society. The vantage-point of the social actors totally determines the cultural item.

Such a theory has many advantages, of course. It gets over the problem of having to analyse anything that might amount to an internal aesthetic. There would be no reason to attempt an analysis of the internal structure and quality of, for instance, pop music. The analysis would be completely social and proceed totally in terms of the qualities ascribed to the artefacts from the outside.

A polar opposite form of analysis would view the meaning and value of a cultural item as totally intrinsic and autonomous. The cultural item would consist, always, of the same immanent qualities. It would keep an essential integrity no matter what social group was responding to it. The first approach suggests, of course, that different social groups could see totally different things within the same cultural item – at least in so far as they had no knowledge of, or no influence upon, one another's tastes. The cultural item derives its meaning from outside itself and is, therefore, different for different groups.

The analysis in the second case must proceed through two stages. First, is the evaluation of the internal structure of the cultural item in its own terms: we might see this as a universal aesthetic. The cultural item would *be* the same, although the profile may alter (as the angle of vision altered), no matter from what vantage-point it was seen. Second, is the analysis of how this structure is interpreted by social groups. There can be no

199

simple elision of codes here, though, and this makes a properly social analysis difficult. The cultural item itself would not simply mirror the social and cultural interests of any social group. It would stand its ground against the contingencies of social interpretation with a universal and unchangeable internal relation of parts and feelings. What particular groups make of it need not intrinsically connect with this.

In some senses, it is easier to imagine cultural items as having an independent objective existence separate from one another and quite apart from their social location. This is an aspect of the commonsense and powerful ideological view of social atomization and random causality which is based on the obvious physical separability of things. It saves us from the work of charting relativism and interdependency. However, this view is basically untenable. The divergence of critical opinion and social response over time, and even within the same period, demonstrate that immanent qualities are less autonomous and 'there' in cultural items than we might suppose. Furthermore the notion of a radical epistemological disjunction between the social group and the items of its cultural field rules out the possibility of a proper social analysis, of any understanding of dialectical change and development.

My position lies somewhere between those sketched above. I argue that the importance, value and meaning of a cultural item is given socially, but within objective limitations imposed by its own internal structure: by its 'objective possibilities'. It is the 'objective possibilities' which are taken up into homological social relationships with the social group. They should be thought of not so much in terms of content, but in terms of structure. Content is really only supplied in the last analysis by the social act and the social relationship. The same set of possibilities can encourage or hold different meanings in different ways. They can simply reflect certain preferred meanings and structures of attitude and feeling. On the other hand, because they relate to something material in the cultural item, something specific, unique and not given from the outside, the 'objective possibilities' can also suggest new meanings, or certainly influence and develop given meanings in unexpected directions. This uncertain process is at the heart of the flux from which the generation of culture flows. The scope for the interpretation or influence of the 'objective possibilities' of an item is not, however, infinite. They constitute a limiting as well as an enabling structure. It is also true that what has been made of these possibilities historically is a powerful and limiting influence on what is taken from them currently.

However, since the 'objective possibilities' are literally *possibilities* – without being quite open they are polyvalent – particular social groups can always find their distinctive form of relation to previously unseen aspects of traditional items. In fact, this is one of the classic constituting mechanisms of minority and dominated cultures. Since the obvious potential for a meaningful relation with important cultural items will already have been exploited by the dominant culture, subordinate cultures have to explore the neglected or unseen possibilities to generate its own meanings. The other important process in the development of subordinate cultures is the creative exploitation of the 'objective possibilities' of new objects and artefacts – provided by the dominant system but not fully culturally utilized by it. Often subordinate groups will seize upon the possibilities of functional artless or narrowly applied items which have been ignored by the dominant culture except for their obvious uses.

3 The integral

Integral analysis is concerned to explain the generation of basic homologies. Where homological analysis is synchronic, integral analysis is diachronic. It investigates the degree to which two elements in a cultural relationship directly influence and modify each other. The 'objective possibilities' of a cultural item – and especially where it is sought out – might be expected to marginally change the sensibilities, structure of feelings and characteristic concerns of the social group involved with it. Now, if the group has no agency to control or reset these possibilities, then this cultural influence is finite. If, however, the possibilities can be changed by the agency of the group in the light of their particular social existence and of the changes that have occurred in the group as a response to its primary exposure to the cultural item, then we can readily see the potential for a

201

dialectical process. Marginal resets in the possibilities of the cultural item produce marginal resets in the social group, which so long as the agency is there, produces further modifications in the possibilities. The direction of change in the possibilities may be instituted by *selection* – that is a more refined choice by the group from among what exists – or by *creation* – the group directly influences the possibilities of new items. Selection as an agent of change (see chapters 2 and 4 on motor-bike boys and pop music) might be expected to be less profound than creation as an agent of change (see chapter 7 on hippies and their music).

The integral level of analysis is basically subordinate to the homological. It historizes the whole analysis and shows how homologies come about in determinate conditions, and also how the 'objective possibilities' of a cultural item are themselves changeable and responsive to human and social agency as well as vice versa. The overall analysis is not, therefore, ultimately, a structural analysis – it does not rely on the invocation of invariant structures – but a dialectical and social analysis.

On the other hand, the dialectic proposed by the integral level of analysis cannot degenerate into an idealist or humanist collapse of the material and human world. There can be no simple fit or identity or harmony between the social group and its cultural field. Throughout the run of an integral cultural relationship the social group is also located in its indexical field and subject to its continuing one-way determination of meaning. This must influence and disorientate the social group even if it finds a contradictory and only ever-partial expression of that very distortion in its own cultural field. The very direction of change instituted in the social group by an integral cultural relationship speaks not only to the internal parameters of this relationship, but is also an exploration and one-sided uncovering of its wider conditions of existence. This is unlikely to be at the level of consciousness or to proceed from conscious intention. It may or may not be 'unconsciously' aided by the particular form of the items these explorations work through – for instance, there is a double relevance in transformations worked through the commodity form. With respect to particular located cultures, there is always a form of 'cultural politics' which links to events and structures outside the culture and which always renders it somewhat decentred to its own proper local concerns. Finally, of course, the cultural field is prevented from becoming a perfect expression of the social group because the 'objective possibilities' of particular items have their own obstinate life. They block certain kinds of meanings, develop others and creatively divert any straight flow of intention.

All these profane factors prevent the collapse of the integral into an undifferentiated unity, as the uncertainly reproduced integral provides a history and dynamic for the homological.

Notes

Preface

1 See, for instance, T. Jefferson and S. Hall (eds), *Resistance through Rituals*, Hutchinson, 1976; and my own *Learning to Labour*, Saxon House, 1977.

1 Introduction: Profanity and creativity

1 I am indebted to Paul Corrigan for this use of the term, 'The Hidden Materialism', cyclostyled paper.
2 Though the phenomenon has not yet become properly unfolded, the same may well be said of the current 'punk rockers'. They show the bleakness of youth unemployment and the nihilism and cynicism of the current atmosphere– the flat plains of recession in the 1970s after the mountainous cultural excitements of the 1960s– much better than unemployment statistics or theories about structural changes in the economy. It is too early to say yet what change they may or may not bring to the situation. For a general account of the phenomenon, see Peter Marsh, 'Dole-queue Rock', *New Society*, 20 January 1977; and the *Observer Colour Supplement*, 29 January 1977.
3 The question of how an object is able or not to hold certain kinds of meaning is discussed fully in the notion of 'objective possibilities' in the appendix to this book, where my position is presented, for those interested, at a more theoretical level.
4 The nature of the 'objective possibilities' of a cultural item also has a bearing on this, see the appendix.
5 See the discussion of the 'selective tradition' in R. Williams, *The Long Revolution*, Penguin Books, 1961.
6 See the debate about pop music and youth culture in *Marxism Today*, for the poverty stricken and undialectical perspective on these matters often taken by the left.
7 The most astonishing example of this process is the development of black music in the USA out of the experience of poverty and from sparse or cast-off musical bits and pieces and instruments taken from the main society. The black achievement in music is enormous, and in particular, through rhythm and blues, underlies all modern pop music.

204

2 The motor-bike boys

1 This style should not be confused with the more recently publicized style of the 'hell's angel'. Hell's Angel groups are much more organized (with a 'President' and 'Sergeant at Arms' of the local chapter'), having a much more complex symbology (death's head markings and signs for having completed daring or odious tasks), have a different style of dress (filthy denim 'originals' instead of leather) and are generally more extreme with a different general philosophy. For a description of the American Hell's Angels, see H. S. Thompson, *Hell's Angels,* Penguin Books, 1967.

2 S. Cohen, *Folk Devils and Moral Panics*, Paladin Books, 1973.

3 See chapter 3, devoted to the symbolic meaning of the motor-bike in the culture.

4 The official reports written by the vicar associated with the club show fantastic death rates (see chapter 3).

5 This lad hung around the club and was generally interested in the motor-bike at a conventional level. He was not a bikeboy, and not part of the culture, though frequently *in* it. For this reason, he proved an interesting sounding-board for many qualities of the culture.

6 In retrospect it is clear that I did not pay sufficient attention to these girls. Throughout the research my attention became increasingly focused on the *masculinity* of the bike culture. This emphasis may have been to partly repeat and uncritically reproduce the boys' chauvinism concerning the women in their ·culture.

7 This report is referred to several times in the main text. It was written by the vicar who had been instrumental in setting up and running the club.

8 As described, for instance, in R. Hoggart, *The Uses of Literacy*, Chatto & Windus, 1957.

3 The motor-bike

1 This and the next chapter will make better reading after a brief review of pp. 1–7.

2 This is the same Percy of chapter 2. He was a 'conventional' motor-cyclist who attended the club regularly.

3 The law, now, of course, prohibits the use of the motor-bike without a helmet in the UK. It did not in 1969–70.

4 This is the report referred to in the previous chapter, written by the vicar involved with setting up the club at which the research was done.

5 The club was on the premises of an old church.

5 The hippies

1 I am following Huizinga and his sense of play here. I certainly do not mean to imply any sense of inconsequentiality in this metaphor. J. Huizinga, *Homo Ludens*, Paladin Books, 1970.

2 This effect arises especially in relation to drug use. It is explored more fully in chapter 6, on drugs.

Notes

3 The following comments bear upon the whole discussion of 'deviancy amplification'. My position, here, however, is somewhat critical of this perspective: it suggests cultural processes which operate in the reverse direction (i.e. for stability) to those posited in amplification theory, and it addresses the question of the cultural content, meaning and generation at stake in the relationship, and of disjunctions between these as they are perceived from the two sides of the relationship.

'Deviancy amplification' theory suggests that mounting hostility between the police and the deviant, and the increased visibility this brings to the deviant act, sets off a spiral whereby the deviant behaviour is exaggerated and progressively defined as more central to their life-style by the deviants. See, for instance, S. Cohen, ed., *Images of Deviance*, Penguin Books 1971; E. Rubington and M. A. Weinberg, eds, *Deviance: the Interactionist Perspective*, Collier-Macmillan, New York, 1968; L. Wilkins, 'Some Sociological Factors in Drug Addiction Control', in D. Wilner and G. Kassebnaum, eds, *Narcotics*, McGraw-Hill, New York, 1965.

4 After the period 'in the field' I contacted the drug squad responsible for this area, and also a local vicar who had done 'caring work' in the hippy and drop-out community. I tape-recorded sessions on their views about 'the scene'.

5 There is a connection here with K. Erikson's theory that society regulates its own criminality in order to maintain 'boundary definition': Kai Erikson, *Wayward Puritans*, John Wiley, New York, 1966.

6 A vicious 'amplification' outlined, for instance, in J. Young, *The Drug Takers*, Paladin Books, 1972.

7 See particularly, S. Hall, 'The Hippies, an American Movement', in J. Nagel, ed., *Student Power,* Merlin Press, 1969.

6 The experience of drugs

1 This and the following chapter give examples of the process discussed in the Introduction. It is a good idea to reread the first part of the Introduction.

2 'Skin-popping' refers to tiny injections of the drug just below the skin. 'Mainlining' refers to injections of the drug directly into a vein. Skin-popping meant that the drug was absorbed much more slowly and was therefore much less extreme in its effects.

7 The creative age

1 Quoted in J. Marks and L. Eastman, *Rock*, Bantam Books, 1968.

2 J. Eisen, ed., *The Age of Rock*, Vintage Books, 1969.

3 In writing this brief section, and the similar section at the end of the chapter on early rock 'n' roll, chapter 2, I would like to acknowledge the help, ideas and advice given to me by Anna-Lise Malmros.

4 For an important analysis of the manner in which modern notions of sequential time are related to industrialization, the growth of capitalism and the bourgeois order, see E. P. Thompson, 'Time, Work Discipline and Industrial Capitalism', *Past and Present*, 38, December 1967.

8 Conclusion: Cultural politics

1 One of the misunderstandings about so-called 'youth culture' has been that it is a classless phenomenon. This belief is actually an offshoot of the pervasive belief in the 1950s and 1960s that class barriers were breaking down under the combined assault of affluence, enlightened social policy (particularly the 1944 Butler Education Act) and general post-war change. In the general context of the embourgeoisement thesis the warning bells were rung by J. H. Westergaard in 1964, and J. H. Goldthorpe *et al*. in 1969. More recently several commentators have insisted on the *class*-based nature of different youth culture: J. H. Westergaard, 'The Myth of Classlessness', in R. Blackburn, ed., *Ideology in Social Science*, Fontana Books, 1972; J. H. Goldthorpe, D. Lockwood, *et al*., *The Affluent Worker in the Class Structure*, Cambridge University Press, 1969; G. Murdoch and R. McCron, 'Scoobies, Skins and Contemporary Pop', *New Society*, 29 March 1973; G. Tyler, 'Generation Gap or Gap within a Generation' in I. Howe and M. Harrington, eds, *The Seventies: Problems and Proposals*, Harper & Row, New York, 1972; S. Hall and T. Jefferson, *Resistance through Rituals*, Hutchinson, 1976. The classless ideology which youth groups *seemed* to support was actually a distorted interpretation of a genuine sub-stratum. Both cultures did share in a challenge to everyday life and the boldness of living through responses and solutions as life-styles.

2 I am using this term in the sense outlined and developed by Max Weber in his classic work, *The Protestant Ethic and the Spirit of Capitalism*, Charles Scribner, New York, 1958.

Theoretical appendix

1 See the discussions of the problems of participant observation in: George J. McCall and J. L. Simmons, eds, *Issues in Participant Observation*, Addison-Wesley, 1969; W. Filstead, ed., *Qualitative Methodology*, Markham Publishing Co., 1970; S. T. Bruyn, ed., *The Human Perspective in Sociology*, Prentice-Hall, 1966. For a fuller critique of these methods and the presentation of my view of the proper use of 'qualitative techniques', see 'The Man in the Iron Cage', in *Working Papers in Cultural Studies 9*, Centre for Contemporary Cultural Studies, 1976.

Index

'mods', 18–21; physicality of interaction, 18–20; and pop music, 35–40, 62–79; 'rockers', 11; security of identity, 13–18; self-reliance and identity, 13; women, attitudes to, 27–9; work, attitudes to, 45–50

Murdoch, G., 207

'objective possibilities', 72, 76–9, 166–9, 193, 198–201, 204; development of meanings, 200; 'double edge', 7–8, 171–2, 201; intrinsic meanings, 199–200; limiting as well as enabling structures, 149–52, 201; reflection of meanings, 200; role in homological cultural relations, 200; socially given meanings, 198–9

participant observation, 11–13, 83–5, 192–8; comparative technique, 195–6, ('autonomous' power of evidence) 196, (bias) 195–7, (cluster of methods) 196, (contradictions) 196, ('triangulation') 196; distinctive problematic of, 194–8; individual, 2, 193–4; naturalistic technique, 194–5, (endogenous and exogenous determinants) 195, (flexibility) 195, (group discussions) 195; role, 12–13, 21, 89, 121, 192–8; self-reflexive technique, 196–8, (commensurate levels), 197, ('empathy') 197; sources of error in, 194–6; status of object, 193–4; subjectivity, 193–4

Pink Floyd, 108, 145, 159

political activity, *see* cultural politics

pop music: and attitudes, 162–4; authenticity and non-authenticity, 154, 155–7, 164–5; beat and rhythm, 67–8; and the bikeboys, 72–3; and the body, 77–8, 95, 99; dancing and, 36–7, 68–9, 156–7; and drugs, 145–8, 161–2; and emotion, 164; electronic techniques, 159, 167; fighting and,

73–5; 'golden age', 63, 64, 71; LPs, 37–40, 63–5, 69–70, 155–6; lyrics 69, 157, 160–1; masculinity, 71; melody, 77, 168; musicological analysis, 76–9, 166–9; mysticism, 160–1, 169; progressive and 'underground' music, 70, 107, 154–69; punk rockers, 204; rhythm, 76, 167; rhythm and blues, 204; rock 'n' roll, 166; social meaning, 66–7; tonality, 76–7, 166–7; 'tradition', 64; *see also* hippies; motor-bike boys

Presley, Elvis, 35, 38, 40, 62, 63, 71, 76, 107

protestant ethic, 90–1, 138, 173–4, 207

rationalism, 172

Reed, Lou, 158–9

religion, eastern, 144–5

Rolling Stones, 65, 67, 71, 158

Rubington, E., 2–6

Simmons, J. L., 207

social group, 4, 170–82, 191–8, 202–3

social structure, 2, 4–5, 170–82, 189, 202; *see also* cultural politics

Souster, Tim, 158

spirituality, 85–90, 143–5, 160–1, 169, 178–9

Thompson, E. P., 206

Thompson, H.S., 205

time, notions of, 78–9, 141–2, 166–9, 174

Townsend, Pete, 158

Tyler, G., 207

Tyrannosaurus Rex, 146

Vincent, Gene, 35

violence, 23, 73–5, 178

Weber, Max, 207

Weinberg, M. A., 206

Westergaard, J. H., 207

Who, The, 156